PRAISE FOR *RECLAIMING HOPE*

"This is an important and extremely timely book. It is partly a memoir, partly a reflection on the relationships between faith and governing power, and partly a road map for navigating the unprecedented social and cultural changes we are facing. It's readable and thought-provoking. Get it, read it, and talk to others about it."

—TIMOTHY KELLER, AUTHOR OF *REASON FOR GOD*

"Michael Wear is a man of deep faith who clearly brought his love for Jesus to his work in the White House. *Reclaiming Hope* offers important insight about his time working in the public square for the legitimate and necessary place of both faith and people of faith in today's political environment, and it deserves serious attention."

—HIS EMINENCE TIMOTHY CARDINAL DOLAN

"This is an important book on many levels: it addresses faith's role in politics and public policy; it reveals Barack Obama's personal faith and beliefs; it calls for Christians to engage in the public square; and it offers hope for America's future. For anyone interested in the intersection of faith and politics, *Reclaiming Hope* is a must read."

—THE HONORABLE MARK PRYOR, FORMER US SENATOR FROM ARKANSAS

"According to my friend Michael Wear, too many of us left the party early! I've known Michael for years and greatly appreciate his commitment to the church and his personal faith in Jesus. *Reclaiming Hope* will certainly give you a fresh perspective on politics—but, more importantly, it may also give you a fresh perspective on faith."

—ANDY STANLEY, SENIOR PASTOR OF NORTH POINT MINISTRIES

"Michael Wear makes a powerfully compelling case for engaging the intersection of politics and religion. Drawing from his personal and singular experience in the White House under the Obama administration, Wear writes a lifeline for these times—that despite any personal differences, hope can unite. The pages in your hand could give you hope and lead and guide us forward as a nation. We can all reclaim hope and carry it with us."

—ANN VOSKAMP, *NEW YORK TIMES* BESTSELLING AUTHOR OF *ONE THOUSAND GIFTS* AND *THE BROKEN WAY*

"As a pastor who has been close to President Obama's personal journey of faith, I was fascinated by Michael Wear's insider account of the events and influences that formed this administration. Surprisingly honest and compelling, this book helps us understand the forces at play in President Obama's leadership decisions. *Reclaiming Hope* will give you a sense of hope for a future we can help shape."

—JOEL HUNTER, SENIOR PASTOR OF NORTHLAND,
A CHURCH DISTRIBUTED

"Michael Wear's reflections on life as a young evangelical Christian working for President Obama are not your typical Washington memoir. There's no 'If only they'd listened to me' bravado nor is there the catty score-settling we've grown to expect from the genre. Instead, this book offers Oval Office insight with road-to-Damascus vulnerability. Whether or not you agree with the author's politics, you can learn what it means to bear witness in a time riddled with culture wars and political strife. Michael Wear is part of why I think a new generation can bring a new shape to American public life, one in which we can disagree without tearing each other apart. We can hope and this book can help us."

—RUSSELL MOORE, PRESIDENT OF THE ETHICS & RELIGIOUS
LIBERTY COMMISSION OF THE SOUTHERN BAPTIST CONVENTION

"In my eighteen years as a leader of the congressional coalition on adoption, I happily witnessed countless times when members of Congress from opposite ends of the political spectrum united behind their shared belief that children belong in families. Revealing such opportunities for common ground was what Michael was uniquely good at. During a time when the political discourse has strayed more to what we don't agree on, *Reclaiming Hope* reminds us all of what can be achieved when we come together."

—THE HONORABLE MARY LANDRIEU, FORMER
US SENATOR FROM LOUISIANA

"More than a story about how faith and politics entangle in the rarified atmosphere of the White House, this fine memoir is also a road map for how we can pick up the broken pieces of our political life and reassemble a national commitment to a common good."

—MIKE MCCURRY, WHITE HOUSE PRESS SECRETARY 1995–98 AND
PROFESSOR OF PUBLIC THEOLOGY AT WESLEY THEOLOGICAL SEMINARY

"Michael Wear's *Reclaiming Hope* is an engaging, sympathetic but not uncritical account of life in the Obama White House. Wear cares about politics, but he cares about his Christian faith even more. The result is a balanced, thoughtful look at how politics and faith intersect, what the pitfalls and possibilities are, and why we cannot give up hope. At a time when too many Christians in public life are discrediting their public witness, Michael Wear is offering an admirable alternative."

—PETER WEHNER, SENIOR FELLOW AT THE ETHICS AND PUBLIC POLICY
CENTER AND FORMER SENIOR ADVISOR TO PRESIDENT GEORGE W. BUSH

"*Reclaiming Hope* is both a fascinating insider's look into the Obama administration's faith-based initiatives and a stirring call for Christians—indeed for Americans of all faiths—to rediscover a sense of hopefulness. Even as we find ourselves in a crisis of disillusionment, and even despair, about the state of American politics, Wear reminds us that we must hold fast to the belief that we can change our country and our world for the better. Each of us would do well to adopt at least a bit of Wear's realistic hopefulness."

—E. J. DIONNE JR., AUTHOR OF *WHY THE RIGHT
WENT WRONG* AND *SOULED OUT*

"This is an unusually important and moving book. *Reclaiming Hope* is a fascinating portrait of a critical moment in American public life, exploring the role of Christianity—and faith more broadly—during the Obama era. Part memoir, part exhortation, Michael Wear offers us an intimate look at the power and relevance of religion at a time when so many have discounted it. The reflections on President Obama's evolution on gay marriage are by themselves worth the price of admission. Marked in parts by disillusion, Wear ends the book with a powerful meditation on hope that, while directed to Christians, will appeal to anyone interested in the complex intersection of faith and politics."

—SHADI HAMID, SENIOR FELLOW AT BROOKINGS INSTITUTION
AND AUTHOR OF *ISLAMIC EXCEPTIONALISM*

"In addition to helping readers *reclaim hope*, Michael Wear's writing and ideas encourage Americans to reframe our views of public service, revive the relevance of civility and religious freedom, and restore the importance of government and faith communities working together toward a common goal."

—JANET VESTAL KELLY, FORMER VIRGINIA
SECRETARY OF THE COMMONWEALTH

"Michael Wear's debut is a warm, engaging read of the author's experience with faith, politics, and the intersection (and sometimes collision) of the two. *Reclaiming Hope* is an important contribution in this age of religious and political polarization."

—J. D. VANCE, AUTHOR OF *HILLBILLY ELEGY*

"Anyone who (mistakenly) believes that the right wing holds a monopoly over faith in America should read Michael Wear's warm and moving account of his work on behalf of Barack Obama—and of the rest of us."

—ALAN WOLFE, AUTHOR OF *AT HOME IN EXILE*

"Transparent. Timely. Helpful. Michael Wear writes with an honesty and impartiality that is rare among politically themed works. Part memoir, part political textbook, part behind-the-scenes glimpse into the nation's most powerful office, *Reclaiming Hope* is a timely and important call for people of faith to rise above the clamor of dissension and work together to make liberty and justice a reality for all."

—LOUIE GIGLIO, PASTOR OF PASSION CITY CHURCH, FOUNDER
OF PASSION CONFERENCES, AND AUTHOR OF *THE COMEBACK*

"Ever wondered what it might be like to be a person of faith, committed to progressive politics, and working at the very center of power? Then read this book. In a world where self-serving and power plays lurk around every corner, Michael Wear's account of life inside the Obama campaign and then the White House is fresh, engaging, honest, and uplifting."

—TIM LIVESEY, FORMER CHIEF OF STAFF TO
LABOUR LEADER ED MILIBAND

"In this wonderful book Michael Wear reports with remarkable candor on his efforts, as an evangelical in President Obama's White House, to get leaders of faith communities and the president's team to listen to each other about some of the most divisive issues of public life. His reflections regarding both successes and failures—along with his struggles to keep his Christian hope properly focused—are fair-minded, eloquent, and inspiring. Michael is one of the young leaders who keeps me hopeful about creative evangelical leadership in the public square."

—RICHARD MOUW, FORMER PRESIDENT OF
FULLER THEOLOGICAL SEMINARY

"*Reclaiming Hope* should be read by Democrats and Republicans, liberals and conservatives, and all who are concerned about the state of our politics. Wear's refreshingly earnest book offers rare insight that just might help us reject the harsh polarization of today's politics, embrace a redemptive faith, and find hope once again."

—KIRSTEN POWERS, *USA TODAY* COLUMNIST
AND CNN POLITICAL ANALYST

"Michael Wear's grasp on how sacred and secular coexist is second to none. His tone is both loving and challenging. A must read."

—PROPAGANDA, ARTIST AND AUTHOR

"In *Reclaiming Hope*, Michael Wear gives the reader a rare look into the behind-the-scenes workings of the White House. Having served early in the Obama campaign, Wear was privileged to go where relatively few Americans ever do, and here he chronicles the importance of faith in the Obama White House. Having served on the Advisory Council on Faith-based and Neighborhood Partnerships and knowing, as a faith-based leader, the intricacies of balancing challenging issues, I can attest to the credibility of this account. Michael is an excellent writer who develops a story and keeps us engaged while giving the reader hope for the potential for faith to impact society for the good. Wear chronicles an exciting yet challenging time and gives us an account that is uplifting. If you are interested in a glimpse inside a presidency and not simply the conjectures of those not privy to internal discussions and decisions, I highly recommend this book."

—FATHER LARRY SNYDER, VICE PRESIDENT FOR MISSION
AT THE UNIVERSITY OF ST. THOMAS AND FORMER
PRESIDENT OF CATHOLIC CHARITIES USA

"In a town haunted by dishonesty and backroom dealing, Michael Wear used his position to serve others, bring people together, and find common ground. Wear's approach to faith and politics is truly distinctive, and in his new book he plants seeds of hope that will yield a harvest of opportunity for a new generation."

—GABE LYONS, PRESIDENT OF Q AND COAUTHOR OF *GOOD FAITH*

"Throughout the course of history, transformational movements have depended upon young people who've been captivated by a positive and hopeful vision of the future. *Reclaiming Hope* is the work of one such individual. For the past eight years, Michael Wear has been actively involved in effecting positive change both within and outside of government. Rooted firmly in an authentic personal faith, he shares his experiences as a public servant and the tensions and opportunities of seeking to incarnate heavenly vision and values. As a result, he challenges us not to shrink from public engagement, but to fully engage the political process armed with an informed hope of and for the future."

—BISHOP CLAUDE ALEXANDER, SENIOR PASTOR OF THE PARK CHURCH

"Endorsing what is good and critiquing what is bad is the main advice on political involvement for Christians given by Michael Wear in these reflections from his time serving President Obama. In delicate but compelling prose this is also what he does of the engagement by the White House with America's diverse Christian communities. Such polite candor helps the reader from 'across the pond' understand the polarization of politics in the US, the divisions in society, and how acerbic the debate has become on religious freedom. Michael's personal account is optimistic on what is still possible in politics. Overall an insightful and enjoyable read."

—BARONESS BERRIDGE OF THE VALE OF CATMOSE AND CO-CHAIR OF THE ALL PARTY PARLIAMENTARY GROUP ON INTERNATIONAL FREEDOM OF RELIGION OR BELIEF

"Several election cycles ago I began calling myself apolitical, even as I advocated for International Justice Mission and went to Capitol Hill on behalf of antihuman trafficking issues. I couldn't find language for both my cynicism and my hope. *Reclaiming Hope* is a gift in this regard—a good theology of politics, housed in a beautifully personal narrative by an earnest believer. I have needed this book for some time. I didn't realize how much I had abandoned hope until I read the last two chapters. Michael isn't on the campaign trail; he is sharing a true hope—not just a slogan or a crutch—that is rooted in a reality that can only be seen with the eyes of faith."

—SARA GROVES, SINGER/SONGWRITER

"A fascinating insider's account of work with US churches on behalf of the Obama campaigns and administrations. Here are both triumphs and heartbreaks: the use of faith to build political support and its marginalization in the daily grind of politics. Wear concludes with a resounding affirmation of the need for Christians to get involved."

—RT HON. STEPHEN TIMMS, LABOUR MEMBER OF
PARLIAMENT FOR EAST HAM, HOUSE OF COMMONS

"Far more than a memoir or a history of the Obama presidency, this is a story of what it is to follow Christ in the most powerful corridors in the world. At a moment in which our political discourse descends into partisan demonization, Michael Wear reminds us of the human face of politics. With his insider's viewpoint, we are shown the realities of the relationship between political life and faith; the disappointments, the compromises, the cynicism but most importantly, the victories and the hope. A fascinating book that will inform, but also educate and inspire those who wish to engage our world for Christ."

—MARK SAYERS, SENIOR PASTOR OF RED CHURCH IN
MELBOURNE, AU AND AUTHOR OF *DISAPPEARING CHURCH*

"This is a captivating book. It journeys with a very young man through the heady environment of presidential campaigns, inaugurations, and administrations. It is a first person account of work in the White House by a person who prioritizes his faith and believes that the choices it drives us to are the ones that will make our country better for all. We can all learn from his journey that even with great good will, our choices are often imperfect. Hope allows us to live this reality more gently and know that our efforts to get it right will make the world better and give glory to God."

—SISTER CAROL KEEHAN, PRESIDENT AND CEO
OF THE CATHOLIC HEALTH ASSOCIATION

"*Reclaiming Hope* is a timely reminder that in politics, ordinary acts undergird extraordinary moments. Behind every policy, speech, and vote lies endless hours of listening, reflecting, debating—even singing. But Wear has an even more important message: each of these ordinary acts is enriched by people of faith, whose continued involvement depends both on their willingness to engage and the willingness of others to engage with them."

—JOHN INAZU, SALLY D. DANFORTH DISTINGUISHED PROFESSOR OF
LAW AND RELIGION AT WASHINGTON UNIVERSITY IN ST. LOUIS

"This book is a fascinating and challenging insider account of the big public religion conflicts of the last eight years and how they might be done better in the future. Essential and gripping reading for those on both sides of the Atlantic about our common life and how we deal with difference."

—ELIZABETH OLDFIELD, DIRECTOR OF THEOS

"If you've ever wondered if you can navigate the corridors of power without losing your soul, *Reclaiming Hope* offers a resounding, 'Yes.' Whatever your politics, Michael Wear offers a hope-filled primer to gospel-centered political engagement."

—REV. DR. GABRIEL SALGUERO, PRESIDENT OF THE
NATIONAL LATINO EVANGELICAL COALITION AND PASTOR
OF THE LAMB'S CHURCH OF THE NAZARENE

"American Christianity has never been monolithic. It is a varied body of young and old, Catholic and Protestant, men and women, gay and straight, conservative and liberal. For some time, I've wondered if there might be a voice that could speak for, and to, this diverse movement. I am now convinced that Michael Wear can be that voice. *Reclaiming Hope* is a riveting read, bursting with insider tales from the Obama White House. But it is also a sweeping survey of what it means to be a Christian in the public square. In a moment where calm and convicted perspectives are being overtaken by divisive, extreme leaders, Michael Wear and this book have arrived not a moment too soon."

—JONATHAN MERRITT, CONTRIBUTING WRITER FOR THE *ATLANTIC*
AND AUTHOR OF *JESUS IS BETTER THAN YOU IMAGINED*

"*Reclaiming Hope* is a window into a millennial's view of faith and politics. Wear reflects on his White House experience and the painfully messy intersection of faith vision and political pragmatism. His evangelical perspective grounds his efforts and challenges readers to reflect on their own experience."

—SISTER SIMONE CAMPBELL, EXECUTIVE DIRECTOR OF
NETWORK AND LEADER OF NUNS ON THE BUS

"Michael is a friend, a mentor, and an example. As my work takes me to the top of political life in the United Kingdom, it is inspiring to have a resource and a guide as full of realistic wisdom coupled with optimistic faith as *Reclaiming Hope*. Beginning as a young intern and leaving as an experienced presidential staffer, Michael demonstrates that Christians can engage with both their hearts and their minds in principled and effective public service. My motto is 'who will lead my country when I am old.' Faith leaders often assume that because I am young I am the answer. Not so, each generation needs to mentor a generation beyond itself and inspire further out than that. *Reclaiming Hope* takes lessons from the White House that will help inspire presidents of the far future. Let that be a message of hope and a lasting legacy of positive politics."

—GARETH WALLACE, EXECUTIVE DIRECTOR OF
CONSERVATIVE CHRISTIAN FELLOWSHIP IN THE UK

"*Reclaiming Hope* is more than the life story of a passionate young leader who used opportunities afforded to him to make a big difference in the lives of others. In allowing us to share in his front row seat to history, Michael Wear challenges us all to look beyond the differences that too often divide us and instead embrace what unites us: shared hope for a better tomorrow. It was this conviction that drew many in the adoption community to him and one of the main reasons why he was such an effective advocate."

—KATHLEEN STROTTMAN, FORMER EXECUTIVE DIRECTOR OF
THE CONGRESSIONAL COALITION ON ADOPTION INSTITUTE
AND LEGISLATIVE DIRECTOR TO SENATOR MARY LANDRIEU

"Essential reading for any European seeking to think about policy and politics that does not enrage people of faith."

—PROFESSOR FRANCIS DAVIS, FORMER FAITH ADVISOR TO UK
CABINET AND TRUSTEE FOR THE UK HOLOCAUST MEMORIAL TRUST

RECLAIMING HOPE

RECLAIMING HOPE

LESSONS LEARNED IN THE OBAMA WHITE HOUSE
ABOUT THE FUTURE OF FAITH IN AMERICA

MICHAEL WEAR

NELSON
BOOKS

An Imprint of Thomas Nelson

Published in Nashville, Tennessee, by Nelson Books, an imprint of Thomas Nelson. Nelson Books and Thomas Nelson are registered trademarks of HarperCollins Christian Publishing, Inc.

Published in association with the Stuart Krichevsky Literary Agency, Inc. www.skagency.com.

Thomas Nelson titles may be purchased in bulk for educational, business, fund-raising, or sales promotional use. For information, please e-mail SpecialMarkets@ThomasNelson.com.

Scripture quotations are taken from the Holy Bible, New International Version®, NIV®. Copyright © 1973, 1978, 1984, 2011 by Biblica, Inc.® Used by permission of Zondervan. All rights reserved worldwide. www.zondervan.com. The "NIV" and "New International Version" are trademarks registered in the United States Patent and Trademark Office by Biblica, Inc.®

Any Internet addresses, phone numbers, or company or product information printed in this book are offered as a resource and are not intended in any way to be or to imply an endorsement by Thomas Nelson, nor does Thomas Nelson vouch for the existence, content, or services of these sites, phone numbers, companies, or products beyond the life of this book.

ISBN 978-0-7180-8233-8 (eBook)

Library of Congress Cataloging-in-Publication Data
ISBN 978-0-7180-8232-1

Names: Wear, Michael R., 1988- author.
Title: Reclaiming hope : lessons learned in the Obama White House about the future of faith in America / Michael R. Wear.
Description: Nashville, Tennessee : Thomas Nelson, 2017.
Identifiers: LCCN 2016036952 | ISBN 9780718082321 (hardback)
Subjects: LCSH: Obama, Barack--Religion. | Christianity and politics—United States--History--21st century. | Religion and politics--United States--History--21st century. | United States--Politics and government--2009- | Presidents--United States--Religion. | Wear, Michael R., 1988- | Presidents--United States--Staff--Biography.
Classification: LCC E908.3 .W43 2017 | DDC 973.932092--dc23 LC record available at https://lccn.loc.gov/2016036952

Printed in the United States of America

17 18 19 20 21   LSC   10 9 8 7 6 5 4 3 2 1

For Melissa

My friends, we have followed the so-called practical way for too long a time now, and it has led inexorably to deeper confusion and chaos. Time is cluttered with the wreckage of communities which surrendered to hatred and violence. For the salvation of our nation and the salvation of mankind, we must follow another way.

—MARTIN LUTHER KING JR.

CONTENTS

CONTENTS

PRELUDE

I would be lying if I told you I was calm and collected. I was twenty years old, it was my first day at my new job, and I was walking toward the Oval Office for a meeting with the president of the United States.

I was not calm and collected.

Of course, I had met Barack Obama on the campaign, but this was different. Now he was "Mr. President." At least, I thought I should call him Mr. President. That is what President Bartlet's staff called him on *The Weswt Wing*. What else did I have to go on?

Long before the sun rose, my first official day at the White House began at the Washington Hilton, where the new president would speak at the National Prayer Breakfast.

The prayer breakfast is an annual event hosted by a Christian ministry, the Fellowship Foundation, that is best described as a relational network of influential government, business, and religious leaders from around the world. Every president has attended the breakfast since Dwight Eisenhower, and Barack Obama addressed all eight breakfasts during his two terms as president. There is not really a comparable annual event in DC that is both privately initiated and yet can virtually assume the president's attendance.

This breakfast was an important event for the president, as it would mark his first time speaking to the faith community directly since taking office. The tone and substance would be closely examined for hints as to how he planned to approach faith issues.

The main, explicit goal of the speech was for the president to announce his plans to revamp the White House's faith-based office. The White House Office of Faith-Based and Community Initiatives was fairly new, created by President George W. Bush during his first term, and it had faced significant criticism immediately and throughout both of Bush's terms in office. Some, mostly civil libertarians and secular activists, viewed the office as a direct violation of the separation of church and state. Others, primarily partisan Democrats and some progressive religious groups and leaders, believed the office was just another mechanism for the Bush White House to reward political supporters. For a while, it was unclear whether the office would continue under the next administration, but Obama confirmed his commitment to support its work after he won the Democratic nomination.

As a nineteen-year-old intern on Obama's 2008 campaign, I could not imagine working in the White House. It was unfathomable. Now, I was sitting just yards from the podium where President Obama would announce his plans for the work that would consume the next forty months of my life.

President Obama, who had always insisted that those in the

blue states also "worship an awesome God,"[1] announced that his renamed White House Office of Faith-Based and Neighborhood Partnerships would be a forum for bringing people together. "Instead of driving us apart," the president said that morning, "our varied beliefs can bring us together to feed the hungry and comfort the afflicted; to make peace where there is strife and rebuild what has broken; to lift up those who have fallen on hard times."[2]

The president had announced his plans for the office at the National Prayer Breakfast, but he would formalize them in the Oval Office. So, bleary-eyed from the day's early start, I headed to the White House.

There are a handful of days in my life that I look back on as days of such promise, such hope, that they are undiminished by all that has passed since—this was one of those days.

I arrived at the security checkpoint in front of the West Wing with members of the newly created President's Advisory Council on Faith-Based and Neighborhood Partnerships. All of the members would stand behind the president as he signed the executive order that would rename and redirect the faith-based office and establish their council.

The president's first faith-based advisory council was profoundly diverse: religiously, ethnically, and politically. Civil rights legend Dr. Otis Moss Jr. joined Southern Baptist Convention president Frank Page; Muslim scholar Dalia Mogahed stood next to orthodox Jewish leader Nathan Diament; Harry Knox of the Human Rights Campaign took part in the council along with Anthony Picarello, general counsel for the Catholic bishops.

As I walked with these leaders up the pathway leading to the West Wing, everything seemed as if it was falling into place.

The president, who had campaigned on bringing the country together, was doing so at one of the most fraught areas of our national experience: the intersection of religion and public life.

A marine stationed in front of the entrance to the West Wing opened up its doors and welcomed us inside. We all marveled to be in this historic building at this historic time, observing the bookcase full of the presidential papers of previous administrations and watching staff power walk past us through the West Wing lobby, off to their next meeting. The famous painting of George Washington crossing the Delaware River accentuated the moment.

We were led by the president's personal staff down a narrow hallway, past the Roosevelt Room on our right, around a corner, and there he was: President Obama. The president had already learned to use the grandeur of his office space to inspire awe and convey power. He stood to greet his guests in the doorway to the Oval Office, a golden, winter light pouring out of the room behind him.

The president shook the religious leaders' hands one by one as he welcomed them. When it was my turn, I muttered something—prevented by a combination of amazement and fatigue from delivering any coherent greeting to the president—and shuffled into the office. As the president delivered informal remarks to the group, I found myself wedged between the wall and a small end table I assumed was crafted by Thomas Jefferson himself. I was afraid to move. I did not want to break the White House on my first day.

He spoke to the leaders about the importance of faith in his own life, and the positive role faith communities had to play in bringing our country through the difficult times ahead. It was a deeply patriotic scene, and I could not help but feel an immense sense of gratitude to be present for it. I felt hopeful, the same way I felt in Iowa when we won the caucus, or on Inauguration Day as the first black president took his oath of office.

But this was different. This was not a campaign speech or a ceremony. This was the president in action—building alliances, enlarging the tent, lifting spirits—actually using the authority of his office to fulfill the promise of his earlier rhetoric.

On that first day at the White House, I was filled with the hope that our politics of division could be overcome, that faith could be reimagined in America as a part of the solution rather than part of the problem. With that hope, I thought, anything was possible.

INTRODUCTION

Hope has been both misused and underappreciated in our time. We have bought into false hope and been disappointed so many times that we have learned to doubt hope itself.

Hopelessness is not entirely new. Clearly, past generations have known it. Aristotle pondered it; the psalmists wept over it; centuries of evil have wrought it. But our hopelessness today is of a different character. We have become closed in on ourselves. Our moral imaginations have shrunk. Our self-confidence, nagged by the suspicion that what we need most might be outside of ourselves, has limited our capacity to dream.

This hopelessness is evident in many facets of our lives. We see it in families, as more young people delay commitment through marriage. Divorce—a legal procedure that formally declares hopelessness—remains high.

When it comes to religious institutions, we have seen an exodus as more Americans self-identify as religiously unaffiliated than ever before. In American religious belief, the gap between the aspirations of our time and our expectations of actual fulfillment is apparent most clearly in the fact that while fewer Americans believe in God, increasing numbers believe in an afterlife.[1]

Hopelessness is also evident in our politics. We know all about the bitter partisanship and dysfunction in Washington, but this hopelessness is not just contained in the sixty-eight square miles of our nation's capital. Our country has the highest number of political independents—people who have checked out of our two-party system of government—in its history. A significant majority of Americans have believed the country is on the wrong track since 2003, leading one journalist to suggest we are in the midst of "our most significant political recession since Vietnam and Watergate."[2] As our culture becomes more political, polarization is defining not just Washington, DC, but our very own communities.[3]

This book focuses on politics for several reasons, the most obvious of which is my personal experience in politics and political institutions. I worked in the White House under President Obama in his Office of Faith-Based and Neighborhood Partnerships during the first three and a half years of his presidency. In my role as assistant to the executive director of the office, I led outreach to moderate and conservative religious believers, including evangelicals, and helped manage the president's engagement of religious leaders and issues. I also coordinated our office's work in certain policy areas, most significantly the child welfare system and efforts to combat human trafficking. In May 2012, I was asked to lead religious outreach on the president's reelection campaign, where I was chiefly responsible for outreach to religious Americans and the campaign's engagement of religious issues. Following the campaign, I directed religious affairs for the president's second inaugural.

One lesson from my time working with the president and religious leaders is that politics is a central influencer of the cultural health of our nation. This book focuses on politics because political institutions create and drive culture, and we can no longer ignore this aspect of how politics functions. As I have talked to pastors around the country, I've come to understand that many of those who refrain from political engagement do so not because they believe it is unimportant, but because they know, for too many of their congregants, politics is important in all of the wrong ways. If we are to reclaim hope, we must understand our nation's political life and our role in it. Politics is causing great spiritual harm and a big reason for that is people are going to politics to have their inner needs met. Politics does a poor job of meeting inner needs, but politicians will suggest they can do so it if it will get them votes. The state of our politics is a reflection of the state of our souls.

One dictionary defines *reclaim* this way: "to bring (uncultivated areas or wasteland) into a condition for cultivation or other use."[4] This book takes that process quite literally.

In the first two chapters, I describe how I came to care about the intersection of faith and politics, and how I met and started to work for Barack Obama.

In chapters 3 through 10, I assess the role of faith in Obama's campaigns and presidency, and what I view as the successes and disappointments of that era. I will recount internal debates, heartbreaking decisions, uplifting moments of transcendence, and nuanced policy successes. As painful as some moments were to live through, and as difficult as some moments are to retell here, they serve to confirm rather than undermine my conviction that people of goodwill, including Christians, need to be involved in politics and the public square.

I tell these stories because in order to move forward, we have to understand where we have been. We do ourselves no favors by avoiding difficulties in the past or understating the challenges and opportunities that lie ahead. This book provides a window into the messy, polarized nature of the way faith and politics intersect today. This book is not a Washington tell-all. I have no scores to settle. I admire President Obama. I love my former colleagues. I respect and appreciate the advocates, clergy, and others I worked with during my time serving the president—even those who disagreed with the president's positions on various issues, even those who disagree with me. When this book critiques people—including the president—it is with my eyes on the future, not the past. We have to know what we want to keep and what we want to clear away if this wasteland is to be reclaimed.

In chapter 11, I will discuss hope. There is reclaiming work to be done here as well, as hope itself has become so distorted in the public mind that it is often either blindly embraced as a motivational tool or dismissed outright as futile. But hope is real. And reclaiming real hope is key to the well-being of our lives, our families, and our politics.

Finally, in chapter 12, with real hope firmly in mind, I will discuss what it means for our politics, and how hope might lead us to address challenges in our public and religious life together.

As a result of my experiences in politics so far, I have convictions about the way forward for our country, and I offer them here with a hope that endures.

CHAPTER 1

FAMILY VALUES

My path to working for the president was an improbable one.

I grew up in the suburbs of Buffalo, New York, in a town and a family emblematic of what writer George Packer has so strikingly referred to as "the unwinding,"[1] the massive social and economic transformation of the last forty years that has led to a hollowing out of America's middle class. When I was seven years old my parents divorced due to economic strain, and so my older sister, Dana, and I were primarily raised by my mother, Genevieve. We did not have a lot of money—my mother worked two and sometimes three jobs for most of my childhood so that we could get by—but I was surrounded by a large, loving Italian family.

The patriarch of that family, my grandfather Jerry, was the man I looked up to, and he was like a father to me. He was a great man. He was an army artilleryman in World War II and fought in northern France. My grandfather was certain the Lord was with him in the war. One night he opened his eyes and everything was bright; his whole area was being bombed. He left his tent and ran across the street to check on the other soldiers. After confirming they were safe, he returned to his tent to find his bed torn to shreds by shrapnel. "No one can tell me there's no Lord," he would say.

I looked up to my grandfather my entire life, and he never disappointed me. I feel a great sense of warmth and security even today when I think of the sound of his electric razor accompanied by his joyful humming of old songs from the army. He taught me through his example about citizenship and community, and about the importance and value of family. It was my grandfather who sparked my interest in public service and politics at a very young age, and those commitments have guided much of my life. Whatever I have accomplished, whatever good I have done in my life so far, is largely due to his towering presence.

He died in the summer of 2005, and I was devastated. I delivered the eulogy at his funeral, marking the end of my adolescence and the beginning of a new age of responsibility. I was seventeen years old. There were so many important decisions to make ahead, and now I had to make them without the one person whose assurances gave me instant comfort.

AWAKENING

I certainly didn't receive much comfort from religion as an adolescent. My family was not particularly religious. In Buffalo, it seemed as if everyone was born Catholic. It was a Catholicism of rituals and rhythms that gave structure to the weeks and years. Religion was "like brushing your teeth in the morning," my mother says: "you just did it." There were Catholics of deep faith in my family when I was growing up, and I have met many more since, but in my youth, religion seemed empty and contrived.

The millennial generation is the first to grow up in a time when religious skepticism is pervasive and accepted in mainstream American culture. Like many of my peers, I internalized messages about religion that I did not really understand myself. I was convinced the Bible was self-contradictory, though I had never read it. I viewed religion as a crutch without interrogating the actual experiences of religious people. I believed religion was anti-intellectual without considering the brilliance of the religious people I knew, or the fact that many of the great intellectuals of human history were religious.

In the same way many in previous generations considered themselves to be Christian because it was reinforced by their peers and culture, I assumed God was unknowable and irrelevant, if God existed at all.

Yet I could not escape God. This God-who-did-not-exist was everywhere.

I have loved rhythm and blues and soul music for as long as I can remember, and it constantly brought me into contact with the gospel. Whether it was a gospel track on an otherwise secular album or the unencumbered praising of God on award shows by my favorite black artists, it was through black music and culture that I felt a sort of tension, a constant knocking that indicated a question that had yet to be confronted stood right outside the doors of my mind and heart.

Then, quite literally, God infiltrated my home. My sister was influenced by a number of high school peers who were devout Christians, and they led her to begin exploring her own beliefs when she was a teenager. Soon enough, she told me she had given her life to Christ, and that I should too. I looked up to my sister in the way a little brother usually does—begrudgingly but undeniably—and so her conversion demanded my attention.

Over the next several years, Dana was persistently proselytizing me. She would give me books, many of which I pretended to ignore but secretly read. She would share with me what she was learning, most of which I initially mocked and later contemplated. One time, she tried to sit down with me and read me something from the Bible and I stood up, started yelling at her, and threw the large Bible back in her face. I found out later that she was praying fervently for me this whole time.

My protestations aside, in my solitude—where there was no one I needed to impress or defend myself against—there was an excavation of all that I thought about religion, about Christianity, and the questions kept turning over in my mind. I read Lee Strobel's *The Case for Christ*, which was a bestseller at the time, and Strobel helpfully deconstructed some of the more obvious, pervasive material critiques of Christianity. I came across a Christian blogger who was gracious enough to correspond with a fifteen-year-old boy who asked difficult, sometimes exacting or obscure questions of him. I exchanged multiple e-mails with the pastor of my sister's church.

In 2002, Lauryn Hill released an acoustic album, a follow-up to her multiple-Grammy-winning debut solo album. The 2002 album merged a theologically rooted political awareness with deeply probing, emotional songs about the artist's personal relationship with God. I listened to the album over and over again, and the intellectual heft of the effort, combined with Hill's emotional sincerity, moved me. In one song, "I Gotta Find

Peace of Mind," Hill sings about how she tried to find contentment in other relationships, but they fell short. At the end of the song, Hill starts weeping, praising God, singing that God is now her peace of mind, and riffing through tears about a God who is merciful and wonderful. There comes a point when the performance seems to end, and it is just her singing to God. I thought, *Something is going on here that is more than just ritual and tradition.*

One evening, after months of saying no, I finally agreed to attend my sister's youth group with her. I think I figured if I attended, I would have more ammunition with which to dismiss her beliefs, but at this point I was also a bit curious.

It did not work out as I had planned: I did not fit in. I did not know the language. I did not understand the culture. One of the girls in the youth group, who was around my age and knew that I was not a Christian, introduced herself and asked, "What is your favorite book of the Bible?"

I, of course, did not have a favorite book. In that moment, I wasn't even sure I knew one. Before I could answer, she responded, "Well, mine is Hezekiah."

I responded hurriedly, "Mine too."

It was only after I became a Christian that I realized that there was no book called Hezekiah in the Bible. She was messing with me.

I did not enjoy the youth group at all.

I endured the event program of music, games, and a sermon. When we were finally dismissed, I told my sister I would be by the car, and I hurried out hoping to avoid another Bible quiz. As I walked through the large, open space of the church's youth center, one of the volunteer leaders with the group was handing out little books. To be civil, I took one. For some reason, I did not immediately discard it. I returned home that evening, sat on my bed, and just stared at the book for a few minutes.

Just Romans. That's odd. No culturally hip messaging? Nothing to try to scare me or woo me? No emotional manipulation?

I read the apostle Paul's letter to the Romans from the New Testament in its entirety that night. The letter contains not just the story of Jesus but an argument about how Jesus fits into the story of human history. Looking back, I suppose that the sensation I had reading that remarkable letter—a letter so extraordinary that while it was written to an entire civilization, it seems to so many readers to have been written just for them—was one of a culmination of learning, a consummation of all that had been working in me those past few years, perhaps even all of my life. But in that moment of rapturous realization, there was a feeling of discovery, of reaching the summit of some majestic mountain-top that I only just realized I had been climbing all along.

Romans is a breathtaking, lawyerly argument about the nature of God, creation, and the human condition. Paul's claims in it are concrete rather than ethereal and he stated them as fact.

As I read, I was compelled to ask the straightforward question I had circled around for years: "What if this is real?" And it was there, at the end of all of my striving to not believe, that I found myself believing. It was there that grace found me.

On an evening in the autumn of 2003, in the car with my sister as she dropped me off in front of our house after school, I told her, the first time I told anyone, that I believed in Christ, "my Lord and my God." To this day, my sister's steadfastness in her prayer and conversations with me is one of the great witnesses of faithfulness I have personally encountered.

Now that I believed, I was not really sure all it signified for my life. What did it mean to follow Jesus? Initially, I thought I had to forget about politics, go to seminary, and become a pastor. What did following Jesus mean if not entering the ministry? After some study and good counsel, I chose a different path: I wanted to discover what faith ought to look like in public.

For a while it seemed to me as though I would have to figure it out alone. I felt isolated as a teenager, but was already beginning to reconcile myself to the idea that my decisions would be mine alone and that I would have to take action alone. This sense seemed to be affirmed as I went deeper into my teenage years.

And then Melissa appeared, as in a vision that seemed like a dream, another reality. She was bold and brilliant—willing to make arguments and defend her intellect. She was utterly unique—we could laugh about the dumbest things, but she never seemed frivolous. She was not flailing about like other teenagers; she was grounded and purposeful. She seemed to be made of meaning.

We began dating before I headed to college in Washington, DC, while she finished her senior year of high school, and we have been together ever since. Melissa has been my reminder that I am not my politics. She knew me and loved me before the campaigns, before the White House, before the fund-raisers and fancy receptions. I would need that reminder in the days ahead.

CHAPTER 2

MEETING BARACK OBAMA

I met Barack Obama not just by chance, but chance that arose out of my own personal error. I was eighteen, a freshman at George Washington University, and I held a position on the executive board of the College Democrats chapter on campus. In that position, I was supposed to lead students to attend the Democratic National Committee's Winter Meeting. The convention that year was particularly important, as it represented one of the few times presidential candidates would have all of the party's superdelegates together in one place. Superdelegates are party leaders who have a vote in the nominating process that can be cast however they decide. They play a critical role in legitimizing a candidacy, and if the race is close enough, they can even tip the balance in one candidate's direction.

This was my first party convention, so while I was excited, I had no idea what to expect. When I arrived at the Washington

Hilton—where I would spend future mornings with President Obama for official events—I expected to see crowds of people and political paraphernalia. Instead, I found an empty hotel lobby.

After twenty minutes of wandering around the hotel, I finally asked the concierge where I might find the convention. The receptionist told me what should have been obvious: I had the wrong date. The convention had not even started yet.

Embarrassed and dejected, I walked through the lobby toward the outside doors. As I neared the exit, I noticed a man whose political career I had been following for several years already and who I was certain would run for president: Barack Obama. Accompanied by only a couple of staffers, Obama walked directly toward me. He had not yet announced his campaign—in fact, his appearance at the convention would be one of the final milestones on the road to announcing just days later. Because he was not yet a presidential candidate, he was not surrounded by hordes of press and aides, and I was able to walk up to him almost immediately.

I stretched out my hand to shake his and began to speak. He leaned toward me, with his ear just inches from my mouth.

"Senator, I'm a Christian who has followed your career for years, and I believe in your vision. I think you should run for president, and I would love to work for you when you do."

Obama smiled and pointed to his personal assistant, Reggie Love, who walked over with an open, small notebook.

"I want you to talk to Reggie. He'll get your information, and we'll be in touch. We'd love to have your help."

"Thank you, Senator," I replied.

I walked to a quieter spot in the lobby with Reggie, and we exchanged a few words of pleasantries while he collected my information. Reggie is a man of imposing kindness. A team captain with the Duke Blue Devils NCAA champion basketball team, Reggie would go on to serve as Obama's "body man," or personal assistant, in the White House. Essentially, Reggie was responsible for the president's needs—as much as any one person could be—24/7.

I was persistent, perhaps even annoying, in my follow-up inquiries and reminders to Reggie and to Joshua DuBois, who covered faith issues in Obama's senate office. My e-mails would alternate between short reminders that I existed and multiple-paragraph e-mails that included campaign strategy recommendations. Looking back, it is hard to pinpoint what it was that motivated me to pursue what was an opaque opportunity.

I had never worked on a campaign before. Would I even like it? Barack Obama was polling in the single-digits for much of the nine months or so I spent trying to work for him. Even if he won, it was beyond my imagination that I could follow him to the White House.

Barack Obama's singularity as a politician was definitely a large part of it. It is undeniable that for me and others of my generation, working to elect Obama became a way to place ourselves in the historic narrative of the civil rights movement. My first explicitly political convictions were related to civil rights, and as a student at George Washington University, I protested in the wake of the police shooting of Sean Bell. I was also involved in the Black Student Union on campus. It was beyond compelling to support Obama's campaign.

My identification as a Democrat did not mean that I was completely at ease in the party. When I became a Christian, I soon understood that throwing myself without reservation behind any party platform was impossible. My allegiances were elsewhere. Politics provided a choice between imperfect options.

I remained a Democrat because of the party's historical commitment to the working class, party members' dedication to combating poverty directly, and the Democrats' leadership in the modern civil rights movement. I was deeply troubled by abortion (discussed more fully later in this book), and that issue made navigating Democratic politics difficult at times. I also disagreed with Democrats' general approach to matters of sex and sexuality, along with other issues. Still, I had profound disagreements with the Republican Party too.

What is also important to understand is that I came of age during a time when the Religious Right had great influence and many Christians were coming to accept that some of the tactics of that movement actually caused damage to the witness of the American church. At the very time I became a Christian, it seemed many of my peers had an increasingly negative perception of Christians. This was in large part due to a presentation of evangelicals in the public square that led many to believe Christians were judgmental, hypocritical, and sheltered.[1] In 2010, respected academics David Campbell and Robert Putnam concluded in their landmark book, *American Grace*, that partisan politics were directly to blame for the rise of religiously unaffiliated Americans. "The growth of the nones," Campbell argued, "is a direct reaction to the intermingling of religion and politics in the United States."[2] Evangelical writer Jonathan Merritt was more blunt in his assessment: "As American Evangelicals have become more partisan, American Christianity has suffered as more shy away from the faith."[3] The evangelical political leaders that dominated political news seemed little like the evangelicals I knew and worshiped with in Buffalo or at my church in Washington. Yet those were the folks who had the Republican

Party's ear. After losing two straight presidential elections, the Democrats were open to just about everyone.

And Barack Obama seemed eager to listen and reach out to Christians like me.

BARACK OBAMA, FAITH, AND POLITICS: A BRIEF HISTORY

There were several novel facets of Barack Obama's approach to faith in public life and politics at the time he was gaining a national platform. First, he was willing to push back against the idea that faith had no role in politics. While other Democrats had ceded talk of faith and values to the Republicans under George W. Bush, Obama forcefully inserted himself into the conversation.

From America's founding to our politics today, Christian ideas are inseparable from any reading of our history or our laws. Religious people have brought their faith to bear on politics, because their faith is what forms their conscience. Barack Obama was not wary of this history. At a time when others sought to remove faith from public life, Obama insisted on recognizing the role of religion in America's history, present, and future.

The second factor was Obama's recognition of an evangelical reawakening to issues of justice and the common good. In the late twentieth century and into the twenty-first, evangelicals increasingly began reaffirming the broad imperative of their faith. People like Ron Sider reinvigorated the evangelical commitment to fight poverty. Gary Haugen helped evangelicals recover the word and idea of justice and seeded the now-flourishing movement to end modern slavery. Bill and Lynne Hybels advocated for immigration reform. Tom Skinner spoke prophetically at an Urbana Student Missions Conference on racism, a forerunner to the evolving conversation evangelicals are now having regarding racial justice in and outside of the church.[4] Even if it wasn't apparent in party politics, twenty-first-century evangelicals were rediscovering the sweeping, broad social consequences of agape love and biblical justice. Obama's engagement with people such as Rick Warren and Jim Wallis indicated he was tapped into this movement as well.

It takes a particular kind of courage and vision to speak about faith as Obama did in the 2004 convention speech that made him famous. As a little-known state senator from Illinois, Obama was not entitled to the national platform he was given that night by John Kerry, the party's presidential candidate. Kerry's selection of Obama to deliver the keynote drew skepticism from many who thought a more established, experienced voice should have received the honor.

Kerry infamously struggled to describe how his faith influenced his politics, and his ineptitude in dealing with religion was one of the primary reasons for his defeat. So it was especially bold of Obama to use the opportunity Kerry gave him to address the intersection of faith and politics. When he argued that alongside our nation's "famous individualism" is a belief that "I am my brother's keeper, I am my sister's keeper," I was sixteen, sitting mesmerized in front of my TV set, just a few years from meeting the man who said those words. When he made the case for national unity and said, "We worship an awesome God in the blue states," disillusioned evangelicals' ears perked up. Countless religious Americans who longed for a more constructive role for faith in politics were motivated by Obama's words to work for his campaigns and administration, volunteer, register others to vote, and reengage in the American political process.

That year, Obama was running against a conservative fire-brand, Alan Keyes, for a US Senate seat. Keyes, a conservative Christian, said in a public forum that "Christ would not vote for Barack Obama, because Barack Obama has voted to behave in a way that it is inconceivable for Christ to have behaved." Obama later wrote about how this nagged at him, as did his dissatisfaction with the response he gave at the time—what he described as the "usual liberal response"—that he was "running to be a US senator from Illinois and not the minister of Illinois."[5]

He would refer to Keyes during a speech at the 2006 Call to Renewal conference—hosted by the evangelical social justice organization, Sojourners—in which he laid out his views on faith and politics in a comprehensive way. In the speech, Obama sought to address the "mutual suspicion" between religious and secular America. Conservatives "exploit" religion by "reminding evangelical Christians that Democrats disrespect their values and dislike their church," and suggest to the "rest of the country" that evangelicals only care about social issues like abortion and gay marriage. Democrats "take the bait," and at best avoid talk about religion, and at worst "dismiss religion in the public square as inherently irrational or intolerant."[6]

He also gave his testimony. In that speech and later in his book, *The Audacity of Hope* (which contains a chapter on faith that is modeled on this 2006 speech), the president begins his journey to the Christian faith with a description and defense of his mother's secularism.

He recounts memories of his mother telling him about "sanctimonious preachers," "respectable church ladies" who were judgmental despite their own "dirty little secrets," and the "church fathers who uttered racial epithets." His mother exposed him to world religions, taking him to a Buddhist temple and a Shinto shrine, just as she "might" have "dragged" him to church on Easter or Christmas. Religion, his mother explained to him, "was an expression of human culture . . . one of the many ways . . . that man attempted to control the unknowable and understand the deeper truths about our lives."[7] His father, who was raised Muslim, was a "confirmed atheist" by the time he met Obama's mother, "thinking religion to be so much superstition, like the mumbo-jumbo of witch doctors he had witnessed in the Kenyan villages of his youth."[8]

Yet, Obama insists, despite "all her professed secularism, my mother was in many ways the most spiritually awakened person I've ever known." She had values "many Americans learn in Sunday school," but she learned them "without the help of religious texts or outside authorities." She had a sense of "wonder," too, that he wrote could "properly be described as devotional."[9] His undergraduate major in political philosophy was part of his "search for confirmation of her values," and it was his search for a practical application of those values that led him to work as a community organizer.[10]

Everyone knows Obama was a community organizer, but what many of those who both mock and praise his organizer roots might be surprised to learn is that his position was funded by the Catholic Campaign for Human Development—an organization funded by the Catholic Church. His work as an organizer was principally with churches on Chicago's South Side that were already helping communities survive in the wake of the collapse of manufacturing jobs in that region.

Chicago might just be the most evangelical, non-Southern city in the nation. It is home to Moody Bible Institute. Willow Creek Community Church—one of the most influential churches in the nation—and Wheaton College are right outside the city. Though Barack Obama was not raised in the black church, the time he spent on the South Side of Chicago, working with churches, the demographics of the city he called home, and his natural ability to understand and connect with people who come from different perspectives equipped him to speak to committed Christians.

It was in Chicago, the rare American city that is a power center for both black and white strands of Christianity (Atlanta is another example), that Obama became a Christian. His experience as a community organizer forced him to "confront a dilemma that my mother never fully resolved in her own life: the fact that I had no community or shared traditions in which to ground my most deeply held beliefs."[11] He also came to understand that "religious commitment did not require me to suspend critical thinking, disengage from the battle for economic and social justice, or otherwise retreat from the world that I knew and loved."[12] And so because of these new understandings, he wrote, he was "finally able to walk down the aisle of Trinity United Church of Christ one day and be baptized. It came about as a choice and not an epiphany; the questions I had did not magically disappear. But kneeling beneath that cross on the South Side of Chicago, I felt God's spirit beckoning me. I submitted myself to His will, and dedicated myself to discovering His truth."[13]

He recounted this personal story at the Call to Renewal conference and said it exemplified why progressives could not "abandon the field of religious discourse." Not only is faith an important part of many Americans' lives, but if progressives ignored faith, "others will fill the vacuum."[14]

The religious role in politics is not just rhetorical, though, he argued, many of the problems we face have spiritual components. For instance, gun violence is not just the result of loose laws but of the "hole in the young man's heart" that leads him to lash out in indiscriminate rage.

The senator summarized his argument in this way:

> Secularists are wrong when they ask believers to leave their religion at the door before entering into the public square. Frederick Douglass, Abraham Lincoln, Williams Jennings Bryan, Dorothy Day, Martin Luther King—indeed, the majority of great reformers in American history—were not only motivated by faith, but repeatedly used religious language to argue for their cause. So to say that men and women should not inject their "personal morality" into public policy debates is a practical absurdity. Our law is by definition a codification of morality, much of it grounded in the Judeo-Christian tradition.[15]

The speech was not perfect: his reference to Old Testament laws against eating shellfish, a trope often used to tritely suggest Christians blithely "pick and choose" which verses to follow, led James Dobson to accuse Obama of "dragging biblical interpretation through the gutter" during the 2008 campaign.[16] While I didn't agree with Dobson's uncharitable tone, that section of the president's speech did not have the nuanced, thoughtful approach to religious questions Obama employed elsewhere.

Still, I was not looking for total theological alignment with a political candidate. Barack Obama understood the religious landscape and historical context briefly discussed here, and he seemed to offer a new way to be a Christian in national politics: confident, but open; conviction-filled, but inclusive; focused on issues of justice and opportunity; and seeking to find common ground in the culture wars, not inflame them.

One of the most important themes of Obama's history with faith and religion is his willingness to assert himself as a Christian voice in Christian conversations. This is central to understanding how he has engaged religion and what his motives have been. This concept is found in his 2004 Democratic National Convention address and in his Call to Renewal speech, along with other earlier faith statements, but his first appearance at Saddleback Church in 2006 most clearly illustrates the point.

Pastor Rick Warren was hosting the 2006 World AIDS Day Summit and invited both Senator Sam Brownback, the conservative Catholic from Kansas, and Senator Barack Obama to Saddleback to show bipartisan support for combating the disease. It was an important moment for Obama: Warren's invitation validated Obama's outreach to evangelicals as something that could be received and reciprocated—even to a Democrat. Brownback surely sensed this.

Brownback opened his remarks by referring to a previous appearance with Obama at the NAACP and juxtaposed their time together at that event with the present occasion. The implication was that the audience at the NAACP were "Obama's people," while the crowd at Saddleback represented "Brownback's people." Brownback finished his story and turned toward Obama, who stood on the podium with him, and said, "Welcome to my house."

The audience got it. They laughed and applauded, many certainly wondering what Obama was doing at a place like Saddleback.

But Obama did a fascinating thing in that moment. Traditionally, Democrats in similar positions—the few that even bothered to place themselves in such positions—accepted this kind of alpha move with a smile or head nod of acknowledgment, an affirmation that said to the audience, "Yeah, it is kind of crazy that I'm here, isn't it?" Just watch the video of Senator Ted Kennedy's appearance at Liberty University in 1983 for this kind of exchange.

Obama was different. With the flash of bravado and confidence that would become familiar—think of his telling Hillary Clinton she was "likable enough," or his 2015 State of the Union rebuttal to GOP applause that he "has no more campaigns to run" by quipping, "I know, because I won both of them"—he stepped up to the podium: "There is one thing I have to say, Sam. This is my house too. This is God's house."[17] In this statement, Obama both affirmed his desire to be placed among evangelicals and asserted his standing to challenge and influence them. We would see the "my house too" Obama again and again over his time running for and serving as president.

THE FIRST CALL

All of this history rushed to my mind when I received the phone call from the campaign in the winter of 2007. They wanted me to come to Iowa.

Melissa was only a couple of months into her freshman year at American University at the time. We had waited a year for this, to be together in Washington, and now I was leaving with no clear timeline of when I would return.

We both knew I had to do it. By this point we were deeply in love; the previous year of long-distance dating had allowed us to get to know each other over the phone and in the letters and e-mails we wrote to one another. We had already decided that we would take on together the challenges and opportunities life would present us.

And this was God's answer to that burning in my heart that led me to Washington in the first place. I had to get off the sidelines and onto the field.

Yes, I decided: I would go to Iowa.

CHAPTER 3

A CAMPAIGN TO BELIEVE IN

The day after Christmas, I joined a veritable flood of Obama aides, interns, and volunteers in Davenport, Iowa, for the closing stretch of the critical Iowa caucus, which would determine much of the fate of Obama's candidacy. The candidate had delivered a campaign-altering speech at November's Jefferson–Jackson Day dinner, a significant Iowa Democratic Party event held just weeks before the caucus, and he had the momentum in the state. Still, he faced the Clinton juggernaut and a talented politician in John Edwards, who had performed well in the Iowa caucus four years earlier.

My plane landed late in the evening, and I headed straight to the packed campaign headquarters. It was past eight o'clock in the evening and staff and volunteers were working dutifully to elect Barack Obama. Immediately, I was immersed in a world teeming with import and purpose.

The run-up to the caucus was exhilarating. For a few weeks,

I was a part of perhaps the most impressive grassroots operation Iowa has ever seen. By caucus night, the campaign had thirty-seven field offices[1] and more than 165 organizers,[2] an unprecedented number of both.

Unlike most elections that are a part of the Democratic party's nominating process, Iowa is a caucus, which essentially means that voters don't simply walk into a voting booth, pull a lever, and walk out, but take part in an event that is one of the most raucously democratic aspects of our electoral system. Caucuses are events that involve speeches, cajoling, socializing, and the counting of votes in real time. Campaigns need to have plans in place not only to persuade voters, but to ensure they're motivated enough and able to dedicate several hours to make their voices heard. I have heard stories of organizers shoveling driveways and sidewalks so senior citizens would have an easier time traveling to the caucus location, and I know of other organizers who have facilitated child care. Organizers and volunteers for a campaign also need to ensure voters are educated and ready to engage with their neighbors since social dynamics can play a deciding role in a caucus.

The personalities of the Clinton and Obama campaigns were on full display at the Bettendorf caucus location where I worked. Clinton's "precinct captains" tended to be older white women who dressed and acted as if they were the hosts at a formal gala. Clinton's campaign posture in 2008 as the realistic grown-up in the race, who sneered at the idealistic naiveté of the eternally sunny John Edwards, and the "hope and change" of Obama, created a culture in her campaign that affected the volunteers she attracted. (In 2016, Hillary Clinton's campaign went to great lengths to present a different face to voters of her campaign's supporters.)

Local Obama precinct captains, on the other hand, were generally younger, a bit overeager, perhaps, but earnest. This was their night; they had labored long hours for almost two years for what would take just a couple of hours. You could see volunteers greet neighbors they had patiently courted for months, and young Obama supporters who practically handcuffed their parents to their side.

The night was theirs.

In a stunning victory, Barack Obama separated himself from Hillary Clinton and John Edwards as the clear winner and instantly turned the "fantasy" of his candidacy into a plausible, even likely, success.

Iowa was a success for me personally, too: I was asked to head to Chicago to continue my work as an intern with the religious affairs department.

A DIFFICULT DECISION

When I first reached out to the Obama campaign, I did not have much of an idea of what it would entail or how I would make it work. When the campaign contacted me in December 2007, I dropped everything and made the trip to Iowa without even a thought about the consequences of the move.

Yet in January 2008, I found myself in Chicago at the headquarters for the candidate who was now a legitimate contender to win the Democratic nomination for president of the United States, and I faced the reality of being a nineteen-year-old college student with no money who was surviving on excess funds from a student loan. I was already signed up for the spring semester at George

Washington University, and though it was possible to get back some of the tuition money, I would completely lose the nearly ten thousand dollars I had already paid for campus housing.

Ten thousand dollars was an almost inconceivable amount of money, and the weight of my decision making was bearing down on me. As much as I wanted to make something of myself and be a part of the campaign to elect Barack Obama, I simply could not put myself further in debt to work for free for almost a year when I had no assurance of what would come next. So I helplessly expressed my hope to staff that I would be able to rejoin the campaign after the spring semester, and I returned to Washington. It could have been the biggest mistake of my life.

What I know now is that these opportunities come once in a lifetime, if you get one at all. After more than a year of trying to get on the campaign, I should have never pulled myself out of it. In the world of political campaigns especially, people move on without you. There are too many things to do, too much pressure, for people to accommodate your needs. If you can't be there when you're needed, campaigns will find someone who can.

The remaining couple of weeks in Chicago flew by: the whiplash of Hillary Clinton's surprise victory in New Hampshire, followed by preparations for the now critical primary in South Carolina, where religious voters would play a key role. I worked long days, as I tried to make the most impact I could with the time I had left.

I returned to college, grateful to be back in Washington with Melissa, but restless and desperate to return to Chicago. We attended the historic rally at American University, where Senator Ted Kennedy endorsed Barack Obama's candidacy. The arena was overflowing, and it was difficult to even get a view of the stage, which was an unnecessary reminder that I had relegated myself to the status of a spectator when I so wanted to be back in the action. I stayed in touch with campaign staff, sending updates or advice based on what I was seeing to try to stay on their radar.

It was during this semester that the Reverend Jeremiah Wright became a focal point of the campaign, prompting Obama to give one of the most powerful speeches of his political career. Obama first met Wright as a community organizer working with churches on the South Side of Chicago. Wright was the pastor of Trinity United Church of Christ, one of the most influential congregations in Chicago, particularly in community development and social advocacy. Wright himself was known as one of the top black preachers in the nation. Trinity offered Obama an important "power base" for his work as an organizer, as a friend and fellow community organizer described it, and a church to call home.[3]

A year after Obama launched his presidential campaign, ABC's *World News Tonight* aired a report on Reverend Wright that featured video clips of Wright's sermons that the Obama campaign did not know existed. In one sound bite, Wright suggested that the 9/11 terrorist attacks showed that "the stuff we have done overseas is now brought right back into our own front yards." Wright suggested to his congregation that "America's chickens are coming home to roost." In another sermon, Wright condemned the United States government for targeting black Americans with discrimination and ill-treatment, rising to say "not God Bless America. God damn America—that's in the Bible—for killing innocent people."[4]

Soon the clips were everywhere. Voters began to wonder

whether Obama's views were more like his pastor's than it had seemed. After all, Wright had officiated Obama's wedding, baptized his children, and inspired the title for his second book. Any effort to put distance between Obama and Wright was difficult, even though as aides told some reporters, Obama was not a regular church attender at Trinity.[5] This was not a problem that could be fixed with campaign statements or surrogates.

On March 18, less than two weeks after the clips first aired, Obama went to the National Constitution Center in Philadelphia to deliver a speech called "A More Perfect Union." After noting that he had already condemned the inflammatory statements made by Wright, Obama described what drew him to the church initially. Reverend Wright was the person, he said, who "helped introduce me to my Christian faith, a man who spoke to me about our obligations to love one another, to care for the sick and lift up the poor." He was a marine, an educated man, and someone who did "God's work here on Earth" through his church's various ministries. Trinity Church itself "contains in full the kindness and cruelty, the fierce intelligence and the shocking ignorance, the struggles and successes, the love and yes, the bitterness and biases that make up the black experience in America."[6]

Obama then skillfully put his relationship with Wright in the context of his own biography and his love of country: "I can no more disown him [Wright] than I can disown the black community. I can no more disown him than I can disown my white grandmother—a woman who helped raise me, a woman who sacrificed again and again for me, a woman who loves me as much as she loves anything in this world, but a woman who once confessed her fear of black men who passed by her on the street, and who on more than one occasion has uttered racial or ethnic stereotypes that made me cringe. These people are a part of me. And they are a part of America, this country that I love."[7]

The speech was broadly praised but did not sit well with Wright, who appeared the next month at the National Press Club and delivered a performance that was, in the words of Obama's 2008 campaign manager, David Plouffe, "divisive, hateful, bombastic, conspiracy-crazy, and just generally repugnant."[8] Shortly thereafter, Obama formally resigned from his membership at Trinity United Church of Christ.

I was proud of the way Obama handled the controversy, particularly his Philadelphia speech. While I was certainly troubled by the tone and content of many of Wright's remarks, I also felt the controversy was aided by journalists' lack of experience with and in the black church—in which rhetoric focusing on the sins of the nation's past (and present) was not uncommon. Nor was I impressed with the Clinton campaign's attempts to leverage the controversy for its own benefit after they had sought the support of clergy and others who respected Wright.

Obama would lock up the nomination in the following weeks.

BACK FOR GOOD

In May, I received an e-mail asking if I would join the team of interns that would stay on through the November general election. This time, I was prepared. I took a leave of absence from my studies. Melissa and I had used the months we had together that semester well, and our relationship was fortified for the time apart. I was all in for the campaign.

The 2008 campaign was one of aspiration, open doors, and new possibilities. There was hardly a voter we did not think we could win, and we would reach out to them all. This included people of faith.

Joshua DuBois, who had worked as a legislative aide in Obama's Senate office before taking the role as the religious affairs director of the campaign, was well suited for the role. He was young—twenty-five years old when we met—and relatively unburdened by the culture war battles, unlike other Democratic staffers. He had held several jobs for Democratic politicians before Obama, but he was not a known quantity, like other progressive faith strategists. He could approach religious leaders as a supporter of Senator Obama, not as a Democratic hack.

DuBois had many qualities that served him well on the campaign, and later in the White House. He was bright, nimble at outreach, and willing to meet people where they were. We would work closely together, perhaps as close as two people could work in a political environment, for almost six years.

In addition to DuBois, there was a formidable faith outreach team in Chicago. I had already met DuBois's deputy Paul Monteiro, a brilliant, baby-faced lawyer and person of deep faith who exuded a confident calmness and striking decency. The staff also included Mark Linton, who had worked in Obama's Senate office and led our Catholic outreach. We would soon be joined by Mara Vanderslice, a tireless and effective politico who led John Kerry's religious outreach in 2004; Shaun Casey, who became close to Kerry following the 2004 election and went on to serve as Kerry's chief advisor on religious issues at the State Department, and several other staffers. Finally, there was a team of six interns: religiously diverse, all kind and talented people.

NECESSARY ADVICE

Early on, I learned a lesson from Paul Monteiro that I will never forget.

I felt in my element from the start on the campaign. This is not to say that I did not make mistakes, or that I understood everything right away, but I did feel that there was nothing I could not understand. My nearly lifelong passion for politics allowed me to have a certain familiarity with many of the key players and ideas at the intersection of faith and politics. Unfortunately, this passion often expressed itself in awkward and sometimes annoying ways. Once, the interns heard a presentation from Preeta Bansal, an accomplished lawyer and member of the US Commission on International Religious Freedom. As Bansal mentioned people and issues she worked on, I would interrupt her informal talk and ask questions, or affirm what she was saying, or somehow express the fact that I, too, was familiar with these people she knew. I was not trying to interject where my voice was not necessary; I simply loved my work, loved politics, and could not contain myself.

A day or so later, Paul Monteiro pulled me aside.

"Have you ever read *Of Mice and Men*?"

I nodded.

"A character in the book, Lenny, loved soft animals. He loved them very much. But sometimes, out of this love, he would squeeze them so hard that, well, their necks would break. He would kill them. You are very good at this work, we are happy with your contribution, and you have a real future in this. But you have to be careful not to kill the rabbit."

It was a graphic, comical, and potentially offensive way to make the point, but it was disarming—it was a critique that I could hear.

I am convinced this advice saved my career in politics before it ever started, and it is about the best advice I have ever received. Paul's advice was also the beginning of my learning how to correct someone while assuming the best about him or her. Paul did not suggest my eagerness came from an unhealthy competitiveness or aggression, or even wanting to stray from my lane, but from my love of my work and the issues at stake.

FIRST BIG MEETING

On June 10, 2008, just a couple of weeks into my time with the campaign, Obama held a historic meeting with evangelical leaders. The meeting was a clear signal that Obama planned to remake the contours of American politics, standing in the gap that had separated us for too long. It was another concrete expression of his forceful rebuke of those who wish to "slice and dice" America along partisan or ideological lines.

In a sign of what would come, there was a little discomfort among some of the president's allies, and even some staff, that the president would hold such a meeting. Despite the fact that it was in line with his rhetoric and the aspirations of the campaign we were all a part of, for some, meeting with evangelicals went a bit too far. One journalist warned, "Obama needs to be more forthright to his more secular-minded supporters about what he's telling religious leaders behind closed doors."[9]

The meeting was held in a downtown Chicago skyscraper in the law offices of a campaign ally. I could not have imagined it then, but the meeting participants included people with whom I would work for the next six years—some of whom would become personal friends. Bishop T. D. Jakes and Franklin Graham were there. Also present were Stephen Strang, publisher of *Charisma* magazine, and his son, Cameron, who publishes a magazine for young evangelicals called *Relevant*; Alec Hill, president of InterVarsity Christian Fellowship (which I attended at George Washington University); Rich Nathan, a national leader at Vineyard USA; and other influential leaders.

The leaders were arranged around a large, rectangular table with name cards indicating their affiliation, with a spot in the middle of the table on the side closest to the door reserved for Senator Obama. He arrived with Reggie and several other staff, and the meeting began. One month earlier I had been taking final exams at GW; now I was one of maybe thirty people in the room for a meeting with the possible next US president and some of the most influential evangelical leaders in the country.

Just the fact that the meeting happened—that evangelical leaders had a voice where they did not expect one, while the candidate was heard by unexpected people—was a victory.

There were two risks with a meeting like this. First, it could have been used against the candidate within his own party. In this case, the odds were particularly low, since Obama held the meeting as he was already the party's presumptive nominee. The second risk was that the participants would say negative things to the press about the meeting—whether accurate or fabricated. But the alternative was to ignore these voters, and that was not consistent with the campaign's identity or interests.

Obama gave brief introductory remarks, and then said that he would go around the large table and allow each person to ask a question. The meeting went relatively smoothly. He received a well-tuned question about how he reconciled his broad perspective that government needed to protect the vulnerable with his position on abortion, and Franklin Graham pressed him on his testimony, but it was the candidate's openness that seemed to leave the most lasting impression. Obama personally understood the people in the room better than any contemporary national Democratic politician. He understood them better than a lot of Republicans.

I was amazed at the whole scene. I had been back with the campaign for only a few weeks, and somehow I found myself here, watching some of the most effective Christian leaders in the nation interact with the person I expected to be the next president of the United States. The meeting came to a close and Obama asked if the group could pray together. I began to lower my head to pray in my seat, when I heard a voice: "Young man, come over here and join us." It was Bishop Jakes. I looked around to make sure it was okay; then I walked up next to Bishop Jakes, and he placed his large hand on my shoulder. I felt another hand fall on my other shoulder; this one belonged to Franklin Graham. We prayed together, Obama shook a few more hands, and the meeting was over.

FAITH OUTREACH AND THE 2008 CAMPAIGN

As the campaign went on, the campaign staff, particularly those in the religious affairs department, began to give me more responsibility as they learned I could be trusted. This trust meant a great deal to me, as I knew that I had very little to lose, and they had their careers on the line. I felt this way through much of my time in politics, even as I became a paid staffer, even as my responsibilities broadened and my input became more decisive.

In a presidential campaign, and particularly in the White House, your decisions are never your own. In politics, you are always acting on behalf of those above you—ultimately the candidate or the president—who will not be able to escape the consequences of your actions. This is why it is problematic, even dangerous, for people in politics to pursue their own agenda separate from the candidate or elected official they represent.

The most important thing a campaign headquarters does is act as a resource to state campaign leadership. After all, we do not elect our president by a national vote, but by winning 270 electors from the states. Unfortunately, in modern American politics only about a dozen states are legitimately up for grabs, which means campaigns only make full investments in those states. In 2008, given the unpopularity of the sitting Republican president and the coalition supporting Obama, we could put about eighteen states in play.

The primary task the religious affairs department had then was to make sure our staff in these battleground states were prepared to engage religious issues and voters. This happened through conference calls and visits to states to do staff trainings, but a key tool that was developed was a state faith manual. This manual included religion-specific etiquette (for instance, when at Catholic mass, "don't take communion if you are not Catholic," or "when attending church services, bring a few dollars to give when the collection plate is passed"), as well as faith outreach program instructions (how to host house parties, for instance); faith outreach materials, like fact sheets about the candidate, contact information for top religious organizations in the state; and a list of people of faith who had already signed up as supporters on our website.

We also had a wide variety of what they call "chum"—campaign merchandise. We received press attention just for the novelty of a Democratic campaign having signs and buttons that said things such as "Believers for Obama" and "Pro-family, Pro-Obama."[10] There was a well-known image of pastors laying hands on Obama in prayer that appeared on many posters and other chum, often including the phrase "I've Got His Back." There was a minor controversy over a placard that said "Christians for Obama" that had a "Jesus fish" on it. The problem was that the Jesus fish was backward, which apparently is a symbol used by some secular groups as an insult. Oops.

One of the most popular pieces of chum, particularly among African Americans, was a church fan that featured a photo of the soon-to-be First Family. In fact, images of Obama with his family had deep salience with all voters. Later, in an in-depth article about the Obamas, the *New York Times Magazine* reported that Anita Dunn, one of the campaign's top strategists, "was reading the newspaper when a voter's quote, expressing surprise that Barack Obama was a good family man, leapt out at her."[11] Dunn shared the quote with other senior advisors, "reinforcing their growing view that he was a more appealing candidate when surrounded by his family."[12] It's astonishing that this was in May 2008, more than a year into the campaign. People of faith were onto the importance of Obama as a family man long before that, and in our conversations with the religious community it came up often. Since then, of course, the Obama family has become iconic in a way unlike any presidential family since the Kennedys.

The goal of our work was to make faith outreach as much of a "plug and play" operation as possible. In some states, we had incredible leadership that was eager to reach out to faith voters.

In others, there was a judgment about allocation of resources, of what kind of outreach was necessary to win, that led to little or no faith engagement. In most cases, these kinds of judgments were political, and certainly within the prerogative of state leadership. In others, however, the decision was not purely political, but flowed from indifference or ignorance. Sometimes—as I came to understand the more I worked in politics—a person's reaction to religious ideas is not ideological at all, but personal. It would surely astound us if there was some way to measure or identify the decisions—political, policy, or otherwise—that stem not from evidence, but that bad childhood experience in church, or memories of a mean Catholic school teacher, or bitterness that God did not save an ailing loved one.

However, after losing two straight presidential campaigns, those in the Democratic Party who urged a more open, inclusive strategy had the leverage over the party's more ideologically strident wing. As columnist Mark Shields observed, "You can tell the health of a party by whether they are seeking heretics or converts."[13] In 2008, we were a healthy party seeking converts.

Other factors gave us new opportunities with the faith community. Disillusionment with the Republican Party felt by many moderate and conservative Christians, particularly young people, resulted in an openness to a Democratic candidate—particularly one without the baggage of fighting the culture wars in the '90s. Barack Obama's ability to reach out and relate to the faith community was only accentuated by John McCain's weaknesses in faith outreach. Not only had McCain once referred to Religious Right leaders as "agents of intolerance," but his campaign was at turns inept and disinterested in persuading moderate religious voters. This became even more clear to me when the leader of a national coalition of evangelicals told me years later that he never even received a phone call from Senator McCain or his staff during the entire campaign.

SADDLEBACK

Typically, retrospectives of modern political history tend to downplay, if not completely ignore, the influence of religion. But it is not insignificant that the only two times Barack Obama and John McCain appeared together during the campaign other than the debates were religious gatherings: the Al Smith dinner—a fundraiser for Catholic social service organizations that presidential candidates traditionally attend—and Pastor Rick Warren's Civil Forum on the Presidency event at Saddleback Church.

The event at Saddleback was just one milestone in a consequential relationship between Barack Obama and Rick Warren. It was a relationship that affirmed both men's best selves. For Rick, it was a public sign of a Christian faith that could bridge all divides, even political ones. For Obama, appearing with Warren not only gave him validation among evangelicals, but even more importantly, it sent the message that Obama's candidacy was for all Americans.

With Paul's *Of Mice and Men* advice still in mind, I did my best to focus on the most immediate work ahead of us as the Saddleback event drew near. However, just days from the event, I was asked to put together several documents in preparation for the nationally televised appearance. The audience for these memos was left a bit opaque, but I approached the project with passion and focus. If I was uniquely capable of doing anything on the 2008 campaign, it was preparing the staff for a sit-down with Rick Warren.

I went to the Christian bookstore near Moody Bible College's campus and picked up several of Rick Warren's books. My task was to provide a summary of *The Purpose Driven Life*, Warren's best-selling devotional, and to anticipate questions Senator Obama might receive and draft talking points.

I put together a five-page summary that described the five purposes laid out in the book ("You were planned for God's pleasure," "You were formed for God's family," and so on) and seven themes the senator could draw on from the book. For instance, one theme was "Christians should be concerned with their neighbor, their country, and the world." Under these themes, I elaborated on how they related to the senator's background or beliefs. For instance, I wrote in one section that "for many Americans, Senator Obama's faith is not only linked to Reverend Wright, but his faith *is* Reverend Wright. Senator Obama should use this forum to define his faith separate from an institution."

I did not know how my work would be used. I assumed the notes would just inform general thinking about how to approach the appearance. I was satisfied to just have that opportunity to influence the process.

On August 16, 2008, I nervously waited with several colleagues for the event to begin. There was no watch party for the event at campaign headquarters as there would be for debates and other major moments, even though this was a singular event. Just minutes before the event started, I received a phone call from DuBois and assumed it was urgent. I picked up the phone.

"Michael, I can't talk for long," he said, "but we just arrived on-site at Saddleback. I wanted to let you know that I had the opportunity to ride with the senator on the way to the event, and I shared your memo with him. He read the whole thing and is deeply appreciative of your work. Thank you for putting that together so quickly. We'll touch base after the event."

I was stunned. I called Melissa right away.

The event had an unusual format: Obama would sit down for an onstage interview with Warren, Senator McCain would join for a photo op, and then McCain would be asked the same questions. The idea was that McCain would be in a "cone of silence," unable to hear the questions Warren asked Obama, but infamously, this came into question in the aftermath of the event.

As the senator walked out onstage, I was nervously scanning my memo. I had put a great deal of care into it, but now that I knew he had read it, my anxiety reached new heights. *What if I wrote something meaning one thing, but he read it as another, and he says something based on my lack of clear communication and we lose the election?* I felt good about how I opened the substantive portion of the memo at least: "Theme 1: It's not about me. It's about serving God and serving people. The first sentence of this section is: 'It's not about you.'" I continued to summarize the themes of the book, and salient points that might come up during the interview.

Just minutes into the event, after the opening question ("Who are the three wisest people you know in your life?"), Warren asked Obama about his greatest moral failure:

SENATOR OBAMA: Well, in my own life, I'd break it up in
    stages. I had a difficult youth. My father wasn't in
    the house. I've written about this. You know, there
    were times when I experimented with drugs, I drank,

in my teenage years. And what I traced this to is a
certain selfishness on my part. I was so obsessed
with me and, you know, the reasons that I might be
dissatisfied that I couldn't focus on other people.
And, *I think the process for me of growing up was to
recognize that it's not about me.* It's about—
WARREN: I like that. (Laughter and applause.) I like that.
(Emphasis mine.)[14]

If I was not hooked by the excitement and grandeur of the
campaign, by the importance of the endeavor itself, I was hooked
now. I had written something just days earlier, and now it was
informing what the leading candidate for the presidency of the
United States was saying in response to a question from one of
the most influential evangelical leaders in the country.

I was too excited then to really think about the implications
of the interview at the time. I read Rick Warren's book, drafted a
document that relayed the key points of that book, and the senator used language from that memo to convey his feelings about
his personal life. And so I failed to ask myself questions later
events would raise for me. Did the "it's not about me" language
simply line up with something he already believed about himself and what he had learned? Or was the language used to build
a false sense of familiarity with the audience? Was it both? In
that moment, I was just happy to have contributed something the
senator found to be useful.

The senator nailed the interview. He seemed honest and open,
and he spoke in a way that was both sensitive to his audience and
consonant with the general tenor of his campaign. His one mis-
step was in response to a brilliantly crafted question by Warren:

Okay, now, let's deal with abortion. Forty million abortions since *Roe v. Wade*. You know, as a pastor, I have to deal with this all the time, all of the pain and all of the conflicts. I know this is a very complex issue. Forty million abortions—at what point does a baby get human rights, in your view?[15]

Obama certainly expected a question about abortion. He had talked about his views on the subject in interviews with Christian media outlets, and the topic was covered in my memo and other briefing materials. Warren understood this, which is why he threw the curveball at the end that moved the question from one of policy to one of principle. Obama, infamously, responded, "Well, I think that whether you're looking at it from a theological perspective or a scientific perspective, answering that question with specificity, you know, is above my pay grade." He then proceeded to respond in a way that was completely in line with his previous answers on the topic, affirming his commitment to leaving the decision up to the individual woman. I knew the "pay grade" response would generate legitimate criticism. It came across as uncharacteristically flippant and did not reflect the thoughtfulness he typically conveys.

Warren had asked a good, smart question. Presidential campaigns have become so sophisticated, so micromanaged, that in the relatively rare moments when candidates are subject to answering questions in an environment they don't control, it's important to try to get beyond the talking points to a deeper understanding of how the candidate thinks and operates. Warren's question helped to do that.

SPRINTING TO THE FINISH

The last two months of the campaign were both tiring and invigorating, with the feeling I would imagine a marathon runner might get when the finish line comes within view. With the exception of the brief surge John McCain received in the polls in the wake of the announcement and rollout of his running mate, Sarah Palin, we were confident we had control of the race. Those feelings and assessments, though, were based on previous experience and previous elections. This election was unique. Campaign pundits wondered aloud whether a significant portion of white voters were telling pollsters they would vote for Obama, but would really vote for McCain on election day, unable to pull the lever for a black man. Our campaign was built around grassroots organizing and turning out first-time voters—largely from minority communities. Pundits and Republican strategists doubted our capacity to do this at the scale we expected, as they would again in 2012. We could take nothing for granted and made extraordinary—and unexpected—efforts to elect Barack Obama.

As noted earlier, from an early age I was drawn to soul music and R&B. As an adolescent and teenager, I would fall asleep listening to *The Quiet Storm*, a radio program format of primarily soul ballads that is typical for urban radio stations around the country. I spent thousands of hours during my youth in my bedroom in front of my boom box singing this music: Blackstreet, Boyz II Men, K-Ci & JoJo, Otis Redding, Alicia Keys, Brian McKnight, Ideal, Maxwell, Usher, Stevie Wonder, and my childhood favorite, Dru Hill. I joke with friends now that when I was young I "hated the Bible, but loved Commissioned [a gospel group]."

Though I gave up the idea of singing professionally when I decided to study politics instead of music in college, music remained a significant part of my political journey. For one thing, it fueled many late nights of work. But it also served as a bridge for me to connect with colleagues and voters.

In the fall of 2008, Donald Miller—the *New York Times* best-selling author of *Blue Like Jazz, Scary Close*, and other popular books—traveled to Ohio for a campaign swing at colleges across the state. One night, after a long day of events, Miller, DuBois, a fellow intern, and I were driving back to our hotel. I was tired, and my guard was down, so when I heard the local radio DJ begin to talk about his nightly countdown of the most popular songs, it sparked something in my brain and I just started to talk:

"You know, I used to call in to my local radio station during these countdowns."

"Oh yeah?"

"Yeah. When I was in middle school I would call up my local radio stations and ask if I could sing on the radio."

"What?"

"It actually got to a point where the local DJ would call me the Sisqó Kid because I would sing Dru Hill so often."

This last fact was followed by shouts of bewildered exclamation and cries of laughter. I had opened up a line of inquiry that would not be shut down easily. After some cajoling, on an interstate somewhere near Columbus, Ohio, I sang the chorus from Dru Hill's "5 Steps."

There was silence.

And then raucous laughter and hand claps.

I was asked if I knew how to sing "Thong Song," the most well-known song by Dru Hill's lead singer, Sisqó, and I let out a couple lines of that song. After more laughter, someone in the car joked, "This is exactly how Republicans imagine a Democratic faith outreach operation: a bunch of folks driving around singing 'Thong Song.'"

Fast-forward to October, and I was in Miami, Florida, focused on the "Get Out The Vote" operation in the state. At the end of a campaign, nearly everyone at campaign headquarters is sent to a state. The large, open campaign office in Chicago became something of a ghost town. Though we had the luxury of not having to count on one particular state to assure our candidate would win—we had multiple paths to victory—Florida was important because it had the most electoral votes at stake of any contested state. Florida also has several weeks of early voting, which provided us with an extended period of time to get our voters—many of whom had never voted before—out to the polls.

These were some of my favorite days on the campaign. I would drive in every morning with Alaina Beverly, the campaign's deputy director for African American outreach, and we would listen to D'Angelo or Maxwell while she stopped by the McDonald's drive-thru for her daily black coffee and orange juice. I was able to meet hundreds of voters, drive many first-time voters to the polls, and visit with clergy and churches across the region.

I still remember Notre Dame D'Haiti, a Catholic church, where I was able to worship one Sunday before the election. Many members of the African American church spoke only French, and we were not able to communicate with one another very well, but I felt so welcomed and loved in that church. An elderly, statesmanlike usher tried to help me find a seat for the service, but I soon realized that the church was packed and so I gave it up and walked to the back of the church.

As I navigated my way through the back of the church, I recognized the melody of a familiar hymn, but they were singing it in French. A member of the parish spotted me, moved by the music, and invited me to look on in his hymnal. My high school French was sufficient to enable me to sing along, and at that moment politics receded into the background.

One night in October, I was driving around southern Florida delivering gas cards to our campaign offices (so volunteers could be compensated for gas used to take voters to the polls), when I received an urgent call from DuBois: "Michael, we're receiving reports that voters are standing in lines that are eight hours long in some precincts, and HQ is concerned. I need you to stop whatever you're doing and meet me."

I protested a bit, as I didn't understand what I could do to make the lines go faster, but DuBois insisted.

You might think I'm exaggerating when I say the wait to vote was eight hours long, but you should know such a wait is common depending on where you live and, unfortunately, how much you make and the color of your skin. Our campaign had staff dedicated to ensuring voters' rights were protected and advocating for expanded access to the polls.

But despite their work, voters still faced hurdles in making their voices heard. Political campaigns have to spend money not just to get voters to the polls, but to make sure that their right to vote is protected at the polling place and that they don't give up if they face a long wait. In Florida and across the country, celebrities who supported Obama would donate their time to visiting the voter lines to entertain people, shake hands, and encourage aspiring voters to hold out and wait. I remember delivering water bottles to senior citizens, some old enough to have paid a poll tax under Jim Crow, who were forced to wait for hours under the hot

Florida sun as they sought to vote for the first black presidential nominee.

Voting is at the very heart of citizenship and of our system of government. I can think of few more significant challenges to hope as it relates to our politics than efforts to restrict voting rights and basic access to the voting booth, particularly insofar as those efforts are tailored to affect specific racial and economic classes of people. These kinds of policies are an injustice that must be opposed all Americans if we wish to claim with full sincerity that we are a nation governed by its people.

I pulled up to the polling site that October evening and saw a long line of voters, almost all African American, waiting to cast their ballots. Then I saw DuBois standing there waiting for me with a bullhorn in his hand. I knew what was coming.

I walked up to DuBois, who smiled and said, "Michael, these folks are tired and bored. They've been waiting here for hours already. We need to find a way to keep their spirits up. So I have this bullhorn, and I think it would be great if you would sing a song or two."

I was never really shy about singing in front of folks. I was in theater throughout my years in secondary and higher education. I performed in talent shows. I would even find opportunities to sing to professional artists, including Dianne Reeves, Blu Cantrell, and Kelly Price. Make no mistake: I am not a great singer. But my voice is just good enough to raise eyebrows and maybe impress folks for a few minutes.

Anyway, there was no use negotiating: I was told the campaign needed me. We stepped up to the voter line, and DuBois made an announcement: "We have a special guest to perform for you all tonight: a recording artist[16] from New York,[17] Michael Wear!"

I nervously stepped up with the bullhorn. I think I was the

only white person there. Folks were justifiably tired and, therefore, potentially irritable. I could think of about eight different ways this could go off the rails. But since there was no turning back, I took a deep breath and started to sing my trustworthy "5 Steps." I remember a group of a few women waiting in line to vote, maybe in their midthirties, and a few notes in they started smiling, moving a little bit, and mouthing the words. I knew then that everything was going to be just fine. Soon enough, most everyone waiting in line was smiling. They all knew the song.

I then sang Sam Cooke's "A Change Is Gonna Come," which Obama later quoted in his Grant Park victory speech on election night. Soon enough, we were having an impromptu talent show. One girl stepped up to the bullhorn and sang the Gershwins' "Summertime." A teenage boy sang a Ne-Yo song. Folks were having fun. They stayed in line. They voted.

I was not able to be on the all-staff call later that evening, but I was told the campaign's deputy director, Steve Hildebrand, had heard about what had happened and used it as an example of why we were going to win Florida.

Election Day went smoothly. We won Florida. We won the Rust Belt. It was a sweeping victory.

It was inspiring to be a part of that night. I never believed Obama would bring about a post-racial society just by getting elected, but just days out from the end of the campaign, it sure felt like a microcosm of the understanding and healing that were so much a part of the narrative of his campaign. Pastor Marvin McMickle reflected on this when he observed that the potential for racial reconciliation appeared "embedded within Obama's campaign structure and strategy."[18] I heard similar observations from civil rights leaders and from regular folks waiting in voter lines throughout the campaign. The possibility for something different felt real to them.

THE MEANING OF THE ELECTION

On October 20, 2008, I had been asked to prepare a call sheet[19] for the senator to reach out to a woman named Ann Nixon Cooper. We learned about her from a CNN report: Cooper had cast her ballot for Barack Obama at the age of 106. In the heat of the closing days of the campaign, the senator wanted to reach out to this woman to thank her for her vote.

I called Ann and spoke with her for a few minutes, and it was moving to hear this woman who had seen so much express excitement for the future. I made sure she would be available for a call, learned a few additional details about her life to include in the call sheet, and said good-bye.

Senator Obama's call with Ann Nixon Cooper stayed with him through to election night, and with millions watching around the nation and the world, he reflected on her life as he gave his victory speech in Grant Park in Chicago:

She was born just a generation past slavery; a time when there were no cars on the road or planes in the sky; when someone like her couldn't vote for two reasons—because she was a woman and because of the color of her skin.

And tonight, I think about all that she's seen throughout her century in America—the heartache and the hope; the struggle and the progress; the times we were told that we can't, and the people who pressed on with that American creed: Yes we can.[20]

The president-elect went on to tell a story of American progress through the lens of Ann's life that went from women getting the right to vote, through the New Deal and World War II, the civil rights movement, technological and scientific advancements, and the 2008 election, when "she touched her finger to a screen, and cast her vote, because after 106 years in America, through the best of times and the darkest of hours, she knows how America can change."[21]

There was a magic to that night, a magic to the campaign, that—for just a moment—revitalized a sense of the possibilities of citizenship. The staffers, interns, and volunteers who worked on the campaign will likely never experience another one like it.

As I will explore later in this book, I believe it is an error to identify Barack Obama—or any candidate or political movement—as the source of our hope. But at the same time, I do not want to dismiss his 2008 campaign as an illusion, to reduce it to a cautionary tale of the dangers of political commitments. There was real promise in that moment. Many hundreds of his campaign staff would say he changed our lives. For thousands of volunteers, first-time voters, and all who felt their voices were finally heard in our political process, the Obama campaign affirmed their dignity.

If only our politics did this all of the time.

WAITING AND HOPING: THE INAUGURATION

For weeks after the election, I heard nothing from anyone associated with the campaign. I was back in Buffalo with family. Melissa was still in DC, finishing up her semester. I went back to my job as a cashier at Wegmans to earn some money.

I knew the staff was tired, catching up with their families and trying to find out their next steps, so I tried to be patient. But I was anxious. I did not know what to expect when I started the campaign, and I certainly did not anticipate or count on it leading to anything, but now I was deeper in debt, and the man I worked for was heading to the White House.

I was at my old high school, speaking to a government class, when I received a call from a blocked number, and I excused myself. I was offered a job in the religious affairs department of the Presidential Inaugural Committee (PIC). And with that call, the skepticism from family members, the financial hole that resulted from the campaign, and the relational sacrifices faded in the rearview mirror. I was going to Washington.

To work on the inaugural committee is to set up a multimillion-dollar operation that you know will last only a couple months. It is fast-paced and, like the campaign, fairly linear with a clear timeline and goal: Inauguration Day. The religious affairs operation for the committee works to ensure key religious leaders and allies are invited to the inauguration week festivities. In addition, the operation deals with the array of religious aspects of the proceedings: invocations and benedictions for the Inauguration Day ceremony and other events, the president-elect's private prayer service the morning of the inauguration, and the National Prayer Service the day after the inauguration.

My eight weeks or so on the PIC went by quickly, as there was much to do, and a tight time frame. I had distant family living in McLean who graciously allowed me to stay in their home for those two months while I figured out my future beyond the inaugural. I enjoyed the PIC work, particularly the ability to connect with clergy. During the campaign, many clergy keep politics at arm's length—for good reasons. But with the election over and Barack Obama the president-elect, engaging with his staff was not necessarily a partisan act.

The first event of Inauguration Day was the private morning prayer service at St. John's Episcopal Church. St. John's is a historic church across the street from the White House, where many presidents have attended. In fact, in 2013, when I was touring St. John's with the Secret Service and church staff, I learned that Steven Spielberg actually sent someone out to St. John's to record their church bell for his movie *Lincoln*. You can hear it at the movie's climax as Lincoln stands looking outside of his window at the White House, church bells across the city ring as Congress votes to approve the Thirteenth Amendment. That same church bell rings from St. John's every day.

These moments were special, and I found them maybe a couple dozen times over the course of my time working for the president. I would arrive early to prepare for an event, pass by tourists at police security blockades, and there would be this space between the people on the outside looking in and the noise of preparation at the event's nucleus: unnaturally quiet, oddly serene, but pregnant with possibility. I could only linger there for so long before I had to head back into the heart of things.

Crammed inside of St. John's were some of the president's and vice president's closest family and friends, and some of our nation's most senior political leaders. It is difficult to describe the heaviness and joy of that morning. There was a holiness to it: these public leaders joining together with the First Family on the precipice of such a life-altering, world-changing afternoon. Just hours from the prayer service, Barack Obama would be handed access to the nuclear football from his predecessor. He would step into the Oval Office for the first time as president, leading a nation on the brink of economic catastrophe and in the middle of two wars in the Middle East.

Bishop T. D. Jakes understood the moment; he preached a sermon on Shadrach, Meshach, and Abednego and spoke of the importance of trusting God in times of crisis. It was difficult to keep my eyes off of the president, though. He seemed to be focused intently during the service. I prayed for him as he prepared to take on the responsibility of the presidency.

Due to security measures, all of the guests who attended the prayer service were transported in a motorcade to the Capitol for the ceremony. After I helped make sure all of the dignitaries were where they needed to be, I hopped on one of the buses in the motorcade.

The city of Washington was essentially shut down. There was no traffic on the streets between the White House and the Capitol except for a motorcade that included a few hundred of the most notable, influential people in the nation: entertainers, politicians, business leaders, clergy, and others. I stared out the window of my bus as we followed the parade route, watching spectators gathered early at the security barrier for the parade line. They held signs and flags, waving at the buses without knowing who was inside. In the seats to my left were Bishop Jakes and his wife, Serita. Ahead of me, cracking jokes to the whole bus, was Rick Warren. I felt as though I were on a school bus heading to a school with an extremely accomplished Type A-only student body.

I listened to the president's first inaugural address, understanding that the speech would be taught in classrooms generations from now. I caught sight—weirdly and unpredictability—of Tatyana Ali, whom I knew as a star of *The Fresh Prince of*

Bel-Air, a couple of rows behind me. And I was moved as the ceremony was bookended by the two American Christian movements that most influenced my life: Rick Warren delivered the invocation, and civil rights icon Rev. Joseph Lowery delivered the benediction.

We returned to the buses after the ceremony and went ahead of the president down the parade route again. I helped Reverend Lowery and his wife, Evelyn, and other religious leaders into their seats. I asked a couple of colleagues if there was anything they needed. I walked around the security barriers to make sure no one was straggling or lost. And then I realized there was nothing left for me to do that day. So I stood next to one of the sets of bleachers at the end of the parade route on Pennsylvania Avenue and waited for the president to make his way to us.

The White House was just behind me, past the fence that didn't seem to provide much separation in light of all of the security that day. The original design of the White House, as I would learn and tell many guests over the next four years, was not to everyone's liking. George Washington believed it was too understated—unfitting for the great new republic he would lead. The residence was expanded at Washington's recommendation and today it stands as a global symbol of American power. It is a destination for millions of tourist around the world who come to the city named for Washington, to visit the president's home and the people's house.

And it is a building of many historical contradictions: Though it was built by slaves, President Lincoln stood by its windows, waiting for St. John's church bells to ring in announcement of emancipation. Burned to a hollow shell by the British in 1814, a rebuilt White House would be witness to meetings between

Franklin Roosevelt and Winston Churchill that would defeat Nazism and save England from fascism. And though the White House was constructed as an idealistic symbol of democracy and self-determination, Martin Luther King Jr. would sit in the Oval Office to demand presidents Kennedy and Johnson act in line with those aspirations. This was the history Barack Obama would step into, as so few have done in our nation's history, to serve the country in the midst of new challenges.

I was thinking about all of this when someone walked up to my side: Martin Luther King III.

"Quite a day, isn't it, sir?"

"Yes, quite a day, indeed," King told me, as we waited for history to march in front of our planted feet.

CHAPTER 4

PRESIDENT OBAMA'S FAITH IN THE WHITE HOUSE

(2009–2010)

In 2016, a reporter asked Jon Favreau, chief speechwriter for Obama since he was a US senator through his first term as president, whether "he . . . or the president had ever thought of their individual speeches and bits of policy making as part of some larger restructuring of the American narrative." Favreau replied, "We saw that as our entire job."[1] This is crucial to understanding how Barack Obama viewed his role as president and his use of the bully pulpit. This is especially true when it comes to the president's policy and rhetoric on issues related to the faith community.

What is the story President Obama wanted to tell about faith in America? In what way did he want to restructure the narrative of faith, specifically Christianity, in the country he led?

No better window exists through which to gain a holistic view of President Obama's perspective on faith and politics than the speeches he gave every year at the National Prayer Breakfast. This is the one annual forum in which the president speaks substantively to people of faith on issues of national and international importance. By looking closely at the speeches, you can get a good sense of what the president is thinking about the role of faith in our nation, and how he wants to influence faith communities.

The fact that the National Prayer Breakfast is held the first Thursday in February is brilliant politics. Every year, just weeks after the president sets out his agenda to the nation in the State of the Union address, he must speak with people of faith at the breakfast. And every four years, just days into a new term, perhaps even a new administration, the president— lest he break tradition—must think about how he will relate to people of faith.

It is difficult to overstate how important this can be. Presidential speeches involve the coordination of multiple offices inside the White House (Domestic Policy Council, Office of Public Engagement, and National Security Council, for instance), and often the involvement of federal agencies such as the Department of Justice (DOJ) or the Department of Health and Human Services (HHS). Speeches force decisions, and they act as a catalyst for action. Once the president says something publicly, advocates, media, and voters can hold the whole government accountable in a new way. For White House staff, what the president says or does not say in public can be used to either push something forward or stop it in its tracks.

The president's decision to keep and strengthen the White House Office of Faith-Based and Neighborhood Partnerships (OFBNP) was not without its critics both outside and inside the

White House. The faith-based office was created by President Bush to unleash what he called America's "armies of compassion." The office played an important role in leveling the playing field for faith groups when it came to partnering with the federal government.

But it faced broad criticism, particularly during Bush's second term.

As the Pew Forum confirmed, media reports on the Bush faith-based office were overwhelmingly negative.[2] Many Democrats and liberals—some motivated by conviction, others by partisan politics—criticized the office as an inherent violation of the separation of church and state.

The office was a source of tension, not just with proponents of a hard church–state separation, but within the faith community as concerns arose about who was, and was not, receiving federal money. As we spoke with pastors and religious leaders during the 2008 campaign, we learned on the ground that there were broad misperceptions about the office and a sense that it failed to live up to its promise. Because of early expectation-setting by the Bush administration that the office would play a role in increasing federal funding to faith-based organizations, many of these groups felt they had been cheated or misled when they did not receive funding.

The truth is that the faith-based office under both presidents Bush and Obama never had a budget for grant making. Under Bush, funding to faith-based groups did not significantly increase, which was noted by the disappointed deputy director of the office, David Kuo, in his memoir *Tempting Faith*. By the end of the Bush administration, the faith-based office was viewed by many as a political ploy at best, and unconstitutional at worst.

It should have been no surprise, then, that some in the White House were not excited that the new president decided not only to keep the faith-based office but to put new energy behind it. I remember one particularly startling exchange.

Early on in the administration, the White House held a leadership development day for young staffers. During one of the sessions, senior staff moderated small-group table discussions. My table was hosted by Stephanie Cutter, someone I deeply admire to this day as one of the most effective communications strategists of the modern Democratic Party. We went around the table for brief introductions, and when my turn came, I simply stated my name, the office I worked in, and the fact that the office helped manage faith-based centers in agencies across the federal government. The second-most senior staffer at the table interrupted me and began a rant about the separation of church and state and what he deemed to be the impropriety of the whole endeavor.

I was stunned. All I had done was say where I worked, and it had provoked an aggressive reply from a coworker, a coworker who I'm sure would have said he served at the pleasure of the president. I was embarrassed to have been spoken to this way in front of my peers, and especially in front of senior staff. My reaction at the time was a feeling of anger, but I did not want to head down that road, so I remained silent.

As soon as I left that table, I reflected on the situation.

Why am I the one on the defensive? Why am I made to feel like an enemy, when it is our boss, President Obama, who made the decision to continue the faith-based office? I have my job because he gave it to me.

THE WORK OF THE FAITH-BASED OFFICE

This internal and external criticism of the faith-based office is important because it shows that from the outset of his administration the president was willing to take hits for reaching out to the faith community. It would not have been difficult for him to dismiss the faith-based office as a vestige of the Bush era—one that most Americans, including many Republicans, wanted to forget. He could have pretended the functions of the faith-based office would be taken up by the new White House Office of Urban Affairs or the White House Office of Social Innovation and Civic Participation and used its elimination to signal in one more way a rejection of the Bush years.

Instead, he revamped the faith-based office and gave it a new name (it was formerly the Office of Faith-Based and Community Initiatives). He also assigned the office four special priorities: "Strengthening the role of community organizations in the economic recovery"; "Reducing unintended pregnancies, supporting maternal and child health and reducing the need for abortion"; "Promoting responsible fatherhood and strong communities"; and "Promoting interfaith dialogue and cooperation."[3] And he included an advisory council of twenty-five of America's top religious and nonprofit experts and leaders.

The OFBNP is unique in that it is the only White House office with a direct management relationship with staff in agencies across the federal government: Health and Human Services, Justice, Homeland Security, Agriculture, and so on. President Bush wisely understood—perhaps the benefit of having a president for a father—that without institutional footholds across the federal government, the office would not have a chance to significantly impact the way government functions.

There was a sense, not without merit, that faith-based organizations faced a skeptical audience in their own government when it came to federal funding. As David Kuo described in *Tempting Faith*, "a bias against faith and community-based organizations existed. In part it was a bureaucratic bias of no particular anti-religious bent." The complicated nature of grant applications, as Kuo pointed out, was a barrier to many smaller nonprofits—faith-based and secular. Much of the bias was just a matter of ignorance; "government officials didn't think faith-based groups were permitted and so tended to exclude them."[4]

The faith-based centers—which reported to both the White House OFBNP and their agency secretaries—acted as advocates for, and resources to, faith-based and secular nonprofits. This structure provided important points of contact across the government for faith-based and nonprofit actors that often don't have the same kind of highly paid lobbyists that advocate for the interests of big business or special-interest groups. Some centers also had a seat at the table for agency-wide decisions that would impact the faith and nonprofit sectors—particularly those that had a strong director or a secretary who valued the faith community.

But parochial concerns are not what motivated those who worked in these centers or in the OFBNP. Instead, it was the daily work of connecting organizations that serve their neighbors to one another and to the federal government. This is the work that made up the vast majority of the time and effort of faith-based office staff. It is not sexy work by any means, but it saved lives, lifted people up, and showed the power of a government that is nimble and humble enough to meet its constituents where they are rather than imposing itself on the people.

The faith-based office exists because of a clear-eyed recognition of the power and centrality of faith in the spiritual and practical lives of many Americans and their communities. Faith-based organizations do not need the government; the government—if it seeks to serve the people, particularly the vulnerable—needs to partner with faith communities in order to get that work done. Faith is a powerful motivator for good. Highly religious people are much more likely to volunteer and donate to charitable causes.[5] Religious organizations such as Catholic Charities and World Vision are the backbone of our nation's social service landscape and the face of American generosity abroad. Few institutions are more valuable in American public diplomacy than World Vision, World Relief, Catholic Relief Services, American Jewish World Service, Islamic Relief USA, and so many other religious organizations that serve abroad, often in partnership with their government.

And at home, it is so often religious people and organizations that are counted on to do the hard work of actually serving the poor, the immigrant, and the outcast. Religious hospitals account for a large percentage of hospital beds nationwide. Religious colleges and universities train up the next generation not simply to grow in knowledge, but to direct that knowledge toward what is good and beautiful. Religious homeless shelters give respite to those with no other place to go. Faith-based adoption agencies help children find safe, permanent, and loving homes.

People of faith often serve quietly, and so their neighbors can be unaware of their contribution, but their contributions are difficult for the government to ignore. Particularly as you get to

the local level, mayors, council members, and other public enti-
ties depend on faith communities to reach where they cannot, to
serve needs that government programs cannot address.

At the end of President Obama's first term, we compiled a
report that tells the story of the faith-based office's work. For
instance, the initiative tackled unemployment through partnerships with local congregations to connect low-income job
seekers to employment opportunities. We know from research
and experience that low-income people often do not have the
types of social networks that can lead to employment, and congregations are one of the few remaining places where people from
different socioeconomic backgrounds are brought together. The
Department of Labor's Center for Faith-Based and Neighborhood
Partnerships (CFBNP) "job clubs" program led more than eleven
hundred congregations to create volunteer-run groups that facilitate networking, counseling, and even training opportunities.

Federally supported school lunch and breakfast programs
feed more than 21 million children each year, but what happens
to those kids in the summer, when school is not in session? The
reality for many children is that they can't get the nutrition they
need to grow and develop during the summer. The faith-based
center at the US Department of Agriculture (USDA) recognized this problem and recruited congregations and community
groups across the country to become summer feeding sites
through the Summer Food Service Program. In 2011 alone, this
center led to an additional fourteen hundred summer feeding
sites across the nation.

The office also launched the President's Interfaith and
Community Service Campus Challenge, which mobilized more
than 200 schools to come together across religious lines to serve

their communities. At the University of Pennsylvania, students of different faiths found ways to help children orphaned during the Rwandan genocide.[6] Students at the University of the Incarnate Word in San Antonio partnered with Catholic Charities to serve refugees from Central America.[7] Because of this initiative, Newman Centers, Campus Crusade chapters, Hillel groups, Muslim Student Associations, and other campus faith groups at schools around the country work together to do good.

The center at the Federal Emergency Management Agency (FEMA) provided trainings and equipped faith communities across the country to be there for their cities and towns when disaster strikes, strengthening community cohesion and helping localities bounce back from natural disasters and other catastrophes faster and stronger than they would be able to otherwise. The center at the US Department of Health and Human Services facilitated community health partnerships that helped expand health care access, stem the H1N1 epidemic, and increase community involvement in local health care systems to boost prevention, lower mortality rates, and reduce hospital admissions. The center at the Small Business Administration opened up pathways to capital for small business entrepreneurs. At the Department of Justice, the center was working with faith-based groups and nonprofits to reduce youth violence and help incarcerated parents stay connected to their kids. The US Agency for International Development center developed a tool to help private-sector donors support relief organizations.

The work of the faith office in the White House and across the centers was not just a matter of statistics; the work was personal to us and to the staff who led it, and it affected individual people. We met and spent time with kids who were no longer hungry during the day because of the summer food service program. Center staff at FEMA were in Nashville after the 2010 flood, and their work helped real people get back on their feet. I had the opportunity to meet countless clergy and nonprofit leaders who benefited from our work and who inspired me with their selfless service to their communities.

Whenever I hear people make sweeping statements about how government is bad and only gets in the way, I think of these stories. I think of the incredible people I met working at the White House, people like Max Finberg, who led the USDA's center after spending much of his career in the nonprofit sector advocating for antipoverty efforts and working to feed hungry people. Or Eugene Schneeberg, who led the Department of Justice's center after running a program in Boston that helped young kids stay out of gangs, and served in government to give that same chance to young kids around the nation. Or Alexia Kelley and Acacia Salatti at the Department of Health and Human Services' center, who worked to support families through innovative partnerships around maternal care, adoption, and fatherhood. I worked with so many dedicated people—too many to name here, but each with his or her own story of public service—who already had stellar careers, and chose to use their gifts and hard work to serve their country.

When people ask me whether Christians can or should serve in government, I tell them about Ben O'Dell. No one has served the faith-based initiative better or knows it more deeply than he does, serving as he did in both the Bush and Obama administrations. Ben officially worked at the Department of Health and Human Services' center, but he was a resource to the entire faith-based initiative, including and especially those of us at the

White House. Ben is exceptionally good at his job and treats his coworkers with dignity and patience. He is caring toward younger staff, myself included, and sought to be helpful in whatever situation God had him at the time. Ben's time in government has helped to show me and many others that we really do make building bridges more difficult than it seems: he worked in a Republican administration and a Democratic administration, and he was deeply effective in both. He did this not through power plays and strong-arming people, but through service and a belief that he had to use his influence and talents to help others. He told me that one of the great honors he had is that he was able to personally thank both presidents Bush and Obama for their leadership. "I could appreciate the weight of the leadership they bore and be thankful for a small but meaningful role of participation in that leadership," Ben told me.[8]

This is the kind of work the president was talking about in his 2009 prayer breakfast speech. Rather than backing out of faith engagement, the president was intent on asserting himself. Yes, he said, "we have seen faith wielded as a tool to divide us from one another—as an excuse for prejudice and intolerance," but we can make a different choice. "The particular faith that motivates each of us can promote a greater good for all of us. Instead of driving us apart, our varied beliefs can bring us together to feed the hungry and comfort the afflicted; to make peace where there is strife and rebuild what has broken; to lift up those who have fallen on hard times. This is not only our call as people of faith, but our duty as citizens of America," he said, "and it will be the purpose of the White House Office of Faith-Based and Neighborhood Partnerships." This was vintage "my house too" kind of stuff from the new president.

The administration did marginalize the faith-based office in some ways. The executive director of the office was changed from the highest level of commissioned officer (assistant to the president) to the lowest (special assistant to the president)—though it is worth noting that the last director of the faith-based office under Bush came in as a deputy assistant to the president. Under Obama, the office's place on the White House organizational chart was also put more firmly under the Domestic Policy Council. This was not without an upside, as it provided a greater institutional foothold to impact policy development, but it is difficult to deny that change influenced how senior staff related to the office, and how the office was perceived by media and stakeholders.

As we have already seen, matters of religion have a way of popping up in ways that often take political leaders and their staff by surprise. An issue of importance to the faith community arises, or a politician unknowingly walks into a religious controversy, and all of a sudden it becomes crucial to have staff who understand the faith community. It is essential, then, to have a strong faith-based office with staff capable of advising the president and senior staff on issues related to religion and religious Americans.

THE PRESIDENT'S TESTIMONY

The 2009 National Prayer Breakfast also served as the forum where Barack Obama would speak of his faith at length for the first time as president. After laying out the mandate of the faith-based office, he confided:

I was not raised in a particularly religious household. I had a father who was born a Muslim but became an atheist, grandparents who were non-practicing Methodists and Baptists, and a mother who was skeptical of organized religion, even as she was the kindest, most spiritual person I've ever known. She was the one who taught me as a child to love, and to understand, and to do unto others as I would want to be done.

I didn't become a Christian until many years later, when I moved to the South Side of Chicago after college. It happened not because of indoctrination or a sudden revelation, but because I spent month after month working with church folks who simply wanted to help neighbors who were down on their luck—no matter what they looked like or where they came from, or who they prayed to. It was on those streets, in those neighborhoods, that I first heard God's spirit beckon me. It was there that I felt called to a higher purpose—His purpose.[9]

Three things are notable about this section of the speech.

First, the president's insistence on affirming his mother's inherent goodness and her status as the "most spiritual person" he's ever known indicated something about his views. His characterization of his mother revealed that he saw those without religious commitments as people with an equal capacity for goodness and moral character. Relatedly, it also raised the issue of whether the president believed Christianity provided any unique contribution to character formation or "spirituality" that could not be attained through other means—at least for some people.

Second, the president's faith is closely tied to the value he saw in Christianity to the lives of the downtrodden, and as a motivating force in the lives of Christians to serve others. It is this personal experience that helps explain his lack of patience for a faith that does not express itself in deeds, a faith that is concerned with dogma or an understanding of salvation, but not action on behalf of those who need it in the present.

Finally, the president's hope for engaging the faith community was made explicit as he closed the speech: "So let us pray together on this February morning, but let us also work together in all the days and months ahead."[10]

2010: FAITH AND THE PUBLIC SQUARE

In the midst of a divisive national debate over health reform, President Obama put faith forward as an antidote to our national discord, and a potential source of civility. The honeymoon phase of the Obama presidency was certainly over, but none of the major faith controversies of his first term had come to a head yet.

The 2010 National Prayer Breakfast speech, as much as any other, reflects the capacity I saw in the president back in 2004. It was the kind of speech that drove me to work for the president and motivated me during the long hours, anxiety, and heartbreak of national politics.

The speech was so good, in part, because it was written in partnership with Adam Frankel. Adam worked closely on the campaign and in the White House with Jon Favreau, the president's wunderkind chief speechwriter. Throughout much of the first term, it was Frankel who would be the person with the pen when the president spoke with the faith community.

I liked Adam a great deal. He is deeply reflective and sincere, and I was particularly impressed by the fact that Adam served as Ted Sorensen's research assistant for his memoir, *Counselor.* Sorensen was the chief speechwriter for President John F. Kennedy, and their work together produced some of the most resonant American political rhetoric of the twentieth century. Sorensen, a Unitarian raised by a Russian-Jewish mother in Nebraska, prided himself on learning and understanding the way Kennedy, a Northeastern Irish-Catholic from one of the most powerful families in America, thought about the world. Sorensen could write in Kennedy's cadence and wrote for Kennedy's voice, not his own. Frankel had a similar talent. He did not share the president's ethnicity or his faith, but he understood how the president thought about the intersection of faith and civic life, and he always delivered.

CIVILITY

In the 2010 speech, the president would argue for the power of faith to break through the cynical incivility that had taken over Washington. The spirit that unites us when there is a tragedy, Obama observed, "is too often absent when tackling the long-term, but no less profound issues facing our country, and the world." He added, "We become absorbed with our abstract arguments, our ideological disputes, our contests for power. And in this Tower of Babel, we lose the sound of God's voice."[11]

Obama went on to explain that partisanship is not new, and we should not "over-romanticize the past," but "there is a sense that something is different now; that something is broken; that those of us in Washington are not serving the people as well as we should." He continued to give an incisive analysis of the cause of this breakdown:

> At times, it seems like we're unable to listen to one another; to have at once a serious and civil debate. And this erosion of civility in the public square sows division and distrust among our citizens. It poisons the well of public opinion. It leaves each side little room to negotiate with the other. It makes politics an all-or-nothing sport, where one side is either always right or always wrong when, in reality, neither side has a monopoly on truth. And then we lose sight of the children without food and the men without shelter and the families without health care.[12]

What is the answer? How can we restore civility? Here, having satisfied the required ecumenical caveats earlier in the speech, the president was straightforward: "Empowered by faith, consistently, prayerfully, we need to find our way back to civility."[13]

This faith-led journey to civility would have three parts. First, a conscious effort to "[step] out of our comfort zones in an effort to bridge divisions." The president said he saw this happening in the conservative pastors who support immigration reform; the evangelical leaders who care about environmental stewardship; the progressives who recognize that "government can't solve all of our problems," and value the role of the family.[14]

Second, we must learn how to disagree without being disagreeable. "I am the first to confess I am not always right . . . but surely you can question my policies without questioning my faith, or, for that matter, my citizenship."[15]

He continued:

Challenging each other's ideas can renew our democracy. But when we challenge each other's motives, it becomes harder to see what we hold in common. We forget that we share at some deep level the same dreams—even when we don't share the same plans on how to fulfill them. Surely we can agree to find common ground when possible, parting ways when necessary. But in doing so, let us be guided by our faith, and by prayer.[16]

This was the type of rhetoric that brought hope to so many that the partisanship of the Bush years could be transcended. The president spoke to how his faith-based office was living out these ideas. "We've turned the faith-based initiative around," he said, "to find common ground among people of all beliefs, allowing them to make an impact in a way that's civil and respectful of difference and focused on what matters most."[17]

He closed with a rousing call to "take up" the spirit of civility, urging those in attendance to remember leaders like Abraham Lincoln, Martin Luther King Jr., and William Wilberforce, who "saw the face of God" in those who opposed them.

A year into his presidency, Obama had not given up hope in the unifying message of his first campaign. He took that message to people of faith. Some responded. In the lobby of the Washington Hilton, not far from where I first met the president, I ran into Os Guinness and Mark DeMoss. Os is a statesman of sorts in the evangelical community, and a longstanding voice for pluralism and civic values. DeMoss is an evangelical communications expert and would serve as my opposite in the 2012 campaign, during which he worked as Mitt Romney's advisor for religious outreach. DeMoss was leading a civility campaign that sought to get every member of Congress to sign a statement of commitment to the principles of civility. Both DeMoss and Guinness expressed their appreciation for the president's remarks, and we were on the phone within days to talk about the civility project. Unfortunately, DeMoss's effort gained little traction, as Congress had little appetite for civility. In politics today, a commitment to civility is viewed by many politicians and strategists as amounting to unilateral disarmament.

HEALTH REFORM AND OBAMACARE

The president's pursuit of sweeping health reform was not a surprise to anyone who followed his campaign. It was a focus of his primary battle with Hillary, the concrete issue that grounded their debate over who would best bring about progressive change. Many of his campaign staffers were drawn to him because of his support for health care reform, including Ashley Baia. Ashley was nine when her mother was diagnosed with uterine cancer. Her mom lost her job, and with it her health insurance, and the family was thrown into bankruptcy. Battling cancer, Ashley's mom worked multiple jobs to keep the family afloat, while the government and health insurance companies did nothing to help. Ashley recalls trying to make her mom feel better by assuring her she really did love relish sandwiches. After a year, Ashley's mom started to recover and Ashley got involved in politics—which brought her to work as a field organizer on the Obama campaign when she was twenty-three. Ashley said she wanted to "help the millions of other kids in the country who want and need to help their parents, too."[18] Ashley accomplished that goal through her work on the campaign, and later in the White House. The president told her story around the country.

The president also told personal stories on the campaign trail about his grandmother, how important her health insurance was in her final days, and what a strain it was for his mother to battle with the health insurance companies while trying to care for her.[19]

Health care reform was central to his campaign. It was the area in which he could have the broadest, most immediate impact at addressing inequality, fighting poverty, and providing security to the middle class. He had to push for health care reform.

We look back at the debate over the Affordable Care Act (ACA) and take its incivility and divisiveness as inevitable and unavoidable. The Clinton-era health care reform battles had become legendary. The 2008 primary campaign and the first year of Obama's presidency were filled with analysis of what went wrong in Bill and Hillary Clinton's 1994 effort at health care reform, and how the Obama administration's effort could avoid the same fate. But even in that fight in 1994, Republicans had been deeply engaged in offering solutions. Many of the solutions Republicans offered in the nineties became centerpieces of the Affordable Care Act.

The process by which the ACA became law was a tortuous one and revealed the entrenched partisanship of Washington.[20] First, the Obama administration—to the frustration of many—decidedly refused to put forward its own detailed plan. The president set out goals—expand access, stem rise of premiums, strengthen consumer protections, and so on—and left the development of the details to Congress.

So with the approval from the White House, Senator Max Baucus—the Democratic chair of the Senate Finance Committee and a moderate from Montana with a penchant for bipartisan deal making—worked to come up with a legislative package in partnership with Republicans on the Finance Committee. Baucus, with the ranking chair of the Finance Committee, Republican Senator Chuck Grassley, formed a working group with three Democrats (Baucus, along with moderate Senator Kent Conrad and liberal Senator Jeff Bingaman) and three Republicans (Grassley, moderate Senator Olympia Snowe, and conservative Senator Mike Enzi).

But as the summer of 2009 wore on, the working group fell apart and the partisan lines were hardened. When the Affordable Care Act was brought up for a vote in December—a plan that from its conception included conservative, Republican ideas, and that was drafted through a process that provided repeated opportunities for Republicans to offer constructive input—passage in the Senate required the votes of all sixty Democratic and independent senators to bring the bill to a vote. Four months later, after the Democrats lost a special election in Massachusetts that cost them their ability to get those sixty votes again in the Senate, the Democrats pursued a novel, though not unheard-of, strategy of passing the legislation through a legislative procedure called *reconciliation*, which requires only fifty votes. Again, not one single Republican voted for the bill.

Perhaps, you might say, these votes were a matter of principle. Even though the bill was modeled on ideas the Republican Party had previously embraced, people *are* allowed to change their minds. Right? And I have many conservative friends, some who supported or were open to Obama in 2008, who tell me with convincing sincerity that it was the Democrats' (and the president's) decision to move forward with reconciliation that broke their trust in the president. I understand that and I appreciate it.

However, even if we accept that Republican opposition was completely rooted in a principled objection to the details of the plan, that does not excuse those who opposed the ACA from attending to the brokenness of our health care system before this plan, and the real benefits of its implementation.

This is the main point I want to raise here, and I raise it as a friend to both Democrats and Republicans, as someone who wants to see both parties thriving. As of March 2016, twenty million Americans had health care who did not have it before. The uninsured rate hit a five-decade low and the percentage of uninsured Americans had fallen across racial categories. According to a March 2015 report,[21] because of the Affordable Care Act, 129 million Americans can no longer be denied coverage because of their health; 105 million no longer face a lifetime cap on their coverage; the rise of premiums has slowed; the cost increase of health care goods and services has slowed to its lowest rate in fifty years; hospital care has improved due to provisions in the law—all of these improvements, and many more, would not have taken place without the Affordable Care Act.

I understand some people's premiums have increased. I understand that some people were not able to stay on their health care plan as the president promised. Their stories matter too, and there are fair and necessary critiques to be made that the ACA failed to adequately address health care costs. I am not arguing here that the law was perfect by any means.

But a mother should not have to lie in bed at night concerned her health insurance company will no longer cover her child's cancer treatments because their cost has exceeded the financial cap set by her insurance. A father should not have to worry that because he lost his job his family won't have the health care they need. A woman should not be denied health care by an insurance company that considers pregnancy a "preexisting condition." These were real problems. The Affordable Care Act helped alleviate them.

It is insufficient to simply reject the benefits of the ACA because it violated a particular ideology or political theory detached from the lived experiences of people. Even if you disagree with the process that led to its enactment into law, even if you disagree—as I do—with certain aspects of the bill, can we at least say that it is a good thing twenty million people have health care who did not have it before?[22] Can we acknowledge that the ACA is responsible for easing inequality by halting, for the first time in decades, "the decades-long expansion of the gap between the haves and the have-nots in the American health insurance system?"[23] Or are our political allegiances and ideologies too significant, too cumbersome, to just plainly acknowledge and will the good of others?

Barack Obama fundamentally expanded our political dialogue to include more room for the consideration of how policies affect others, not just ourselves. He is the politician who injected the phrase "I am my brother's keeper" into the political lexicon.

The president understood when he gave his 2010 prayer breakfast speech, as we should understand now, that politics deeply influences our public square. We cannot separate the two. We cannot expect a public square that reflects our values if we ignore our politics—they are too closely tied, too dependent on one another.

CHAPTER 5

PRESIDENT OBAMA'S FAITH IN THE WHITE HOUSE

(2011–2012)

Barack Obama's presidency looked drastically different at the start of 2011 than it had a year earlier. He had accomplished much, including ushering the Affordable Care Act into law, finally achieving the goal of sweeping health reform that Democrats had pursued for decades. And though the administration was not declaring it just yet, we were also confident that economic catastrophe had been prevented—and furthermore, that the American economy was poised for a comeback.

And yet, the president's call for a return to the "spirit of civility," which he had made a year earlier in his prayer breakfast speech, seemed in 2011 to be little more than an instance of gallows humor. The passage of the Affordable Care Act came at the cost of a conservative uprising that hounded Democrats throughout the summer (and cost them the majority in the House of Representatives that fall). Subsequently, the Pew Forum came out with new numbers that showed that a significant portion of Americans continued to believe, or at least reported they believed, that the president was Muslim.[1]

The new year would bring controversy and tension with the religious community that would irrevocably change how people of faith related to the president: less than a month after the 2011 prayer breakfast, Attorney General Eric Holder would announce the Department of Justice would no longer defend the Defense of Marriage Act in court.

So it was in this context of a new Republican Congress, increasing cynicism and division in our politics, and a narrative of uncertainty about the faith of the most well-known American in the world that the president went to the National Prayer Breakfast to give something of a personal testimony.

THE PRESIDENT GETS PERSONAL

The persistence of doubt and flat-out mischaracterization of the president's faith and views on faith in public life was sometimes aided by the president himself. In April 2008—just a month after his famous race speech that calmed the waters from the Reverend Wright controversy—Senator[2] Obama offered his analysis on why he was losing working-class white voters, observing that people in "small towns in Pennsylvania [and] the Midwest" saw their economic prospects decline under the Clinton and Bush administrations, and whenever that happens "they get bitter, they cling to guns or religion or antipathy to people who aren't like them or anti-immigrant sentiment or anti-trade sentiment as a way to explain their frustrations."[3]

These remarks were made in front of wealthy donors in San Francisco, which only highlighted the elitism of the sentiments.

David Plouffe, the president's campaign manager in 2008, later wrote, "I couldn't imagine a worse context for him to have made such boneheaded comments: standing in a room full of wealthy donors in San Francisco—to much of the country a culturally extreme and elitist city with far-out views—speaking in anthropological terms about the middle of the country; describing the setting, it really couldn't sound much worse."[4]

Obama, on the phone with Plouffe soon after he made the comment, admitted that "it should be clear what I was trying to say . . . But I really did mangle the words. It didn't dawn on me at the time that I had misspoken, but looking at the transcript now, I really don't know how the hell I constructed my point like that."[5]

For those Christians who were tired of President Bush and the Religious Right and had hoped Obama was a different kind of Democrat, the comment was enough to give them pause. The campaign's hope was that Obama had connected with voters strongly enough that they would give him a second chance. In his book, Plouffe recounts something he overheard in an airport bar soon after the remark was made public:

The Pittsburgh Penguins game was on, and in between some cheers and boos I picked up a conversation about "Bittergate," which was just in its infancy. The gist of it went like this:

"So maybe this is who he is after all," a guy at the bar said to his buddy sitting next to him. "He hid it for a while, but now we see he looks down on us if we hunt, go to church, lead normal lives. Just like the rest of the Democrats."

"Maybe, but maybe he just messed up," his friend replied. "It doesn't sound like him. I'm going to put him on probation."[6]

Over the course of his administration, many voters—even those who had forgiven these remarks and voted for the president in 2008—would think back on these comments when the president took a policy action or made a comment they considered discordant with a Christian worldview and wonder if "maybe that was who he is after all."

The other sensible, fact-based ground for questioning the sincerity of the president's faith was the fact that he didn't belong to a church in Washington. Journalists often speculated the reason for this was a sort of political aversion to being tied to one church after the controversy involving Trinity and Reverend Wright, but I don't think that was the predominant factor.

In fact, while the president felt burned by Wright, particularly following his egregious appearance at the National Press Club, I think the most powerful lesson from that experience is that by the very nature of our politics, it is the congregation that is made vulnerable by attachment to a national politician. Think about it: how would you feel if your church was in the news, characterized by pundits who might not share your faith and never stepped inside your church?

I also know that there was thoughtful consideration of joining a church. I know this because one of the very first tasks I received as a White House staffer was to scope out church options for the First Family.

I took the job seriously, not just as an appointee serving the president of the United States, but as a Christian who believes the local church is important. I put together a list of about a dozen churches and visited them all in one weekend in a rented car. It was surreal to drive around downtown DC on a quiet weekend morning, visiting churches where the First Family would potentially attend and grow in faith. I would take notes on the churches that I thought would be important for staff to know, or for the First Family to consider.

Has a vibrant kids ministry.
Frederick Douglass worshipped at this church.
Church layout might pose security challenges.
Their church choir is really good.[7]
Beautiful, welcoming sanctuary.

The resulting memo was given to the president, but the family ultimately chose not to join a church. Nevertheless, they did visit many of the churches over the course of his time in office.

One reason for the decision was that it was genuinely disruptive for the president to attend church. We learned this lesson early on, before he even moved to the White House.

On January 18, 2009, the First Family was set to attend the Nineteenth Street Baptist Church. The visit was an opportunity for them to attend church before the president's inauguration, but it was also the first sort of test run, an opportunity for them to try a church they might like in the area.

The first lesson of taking the president to church is that it is a logistical nightmare. The trips, like all presidential travel and events, involved coordination between communications staff, advance staff, the Secret Service, and other relevant departments. These various departments would meet at the church with church staff at least once before the service.

The Secret Service would evaluate the security of the building: Where is the safest place for the president's motorcade to arrive and depart? Where is the safest place for the First Family to sit? Does the church service require the First Family to move from their seats? Do church services typically involve other congregants moving from their seats (think charismatic worship, communion, and so on)?

But it wasn't just the staff coordination on our end that was an issue. We would have sacrificed whatever it took if it meant the First Family could attend church when they wanted. It was the strain on the church that was problematic.

When the First Family attends your church service, it is no longer just a church service, but a presidential event. We did not fully understand this until the Nineteenth Street Baptist Church visit. Due to security measures, the church is typically not able to notify their members of their special guests until just days before the service. When members are notified, it is to tell them that they will have to arrive to church hours early in order to go through magnetometers and have their purses and bags screened. Everyone in the church must arrive by a certain time before the doors are closed and secured. The pastor must announce protocol for the service, including that worship might be restricted ("no running down the aisles, please!"), and that everyone should stay seated until the president and his family leave the building. Of course, the pastor will have plenty of time to repeat this guidance, because the congregation will have to be seated long before the service even starts.

This brings us to the second lesson of taking the president to church: it harms the worship—for the church and for the president and his family. The experience at Nineteenth Street Baptist

Church, as gracious and vibrant a church as it is, taught us this lesson vividly. Since the president can't just "show up" at church, it is not uncommon for word to spread. And by "spread," I mean, "end up in the *Washington Post.*" This is what happened with that first visit. A *Washington Post* reporter heard from a contact at the church that the president would be attending, and the news broke Saturday evening. Sunday morning, not only were members of the church waiting in line to get in, but tourists. Many, many tourists. They were easy to spot because Nineteenth Street Baptist is a traditional, historically black congregation where it was customary for church members to come dressed in dapper suits and beautiful "church lady" hats. I could only conclude that the white gentleman in a Hawaiian shirt, khakis, and sneakers was not a weekly congregant. The influx of tourists meant that members of Nineteenth Street—who only wanted to worship and would have been there regardless of the president's attendance— were displaced.

Once the First Family arrives, and the press pool finds their place in the reserved rows in the back of the congregation,[8] the service can start. But the service is no longer focused on the worship music the choir is providing, or the sermon the pastor is giving, but how the president is responding to the service. Is he singing? Did he nod his head at that line? Did he nod his head because he thought what the pastor said was right? Or did it hit him hard personally? Was that a nod of repentance? What does it mean for the fate of the country that the president nodded at that line?

If you search for photos of the Obama family at church, one in particular comes up right away. The photo is iconic, particularly for African American Christians who saw in the photo their faith, race, and history tied up in one single image. In the photo, the First Family is kneeling at the altar, preparing to take the Eucharist. It is stunning: the president's elegant hands folded in humility. The First Lady's head bowed, enhancing her fierce grace. Malia in solemn prayer, matching her parents, calming fears I've heard from some Christians that the Obamas' daughters were not being brought up in the faith. Sasha, kneeling next to her sister, hands folded, staring off, taking it all in. The whole family is drenched in light coming in through a stained-glass window. The picture has this striking purity about it.

Zoom out, and the picture would likely reflect more selfie than sacrament. You'd see the First Family walking down the aisle, cameras flashing in their faces, people bumping into one another to try and get the frame just right, every pair of eyes in the congregation on them. People saying genuinely encouraging, but equally distracting, words to the First Family as they pass. As the First Family kneels, the pictures continue, journalists tweet, oglers ogle.

I do not mean to disparage at all the churches or the congregations the president visited. The First Family felt welcomed in each one; they were all gracious hosts. But the weight of the presidency fundamentally alters worship in a church.[9]

Still, the First Family attended church services more than a dozen times during the first term, more often than President Reagan.[10] They would attend area African American congregations, or St. John's Episcopal Church across the street, where many presidents have attended—including Lincoln and George W. Bush. The First Family also attended the chapel at Camp David, which was pastored by a Southern Baptist chaplain, Carey Cash.

In lieu of joining a local church, we considered the option of holding private services in the White House, as President Nixon had sometimes done. I do not know why the First Family decided against doing so, but I did not need nor did I have a right to know. Nor does anyone else.

A flippancy concerning the president's faith was not uncommon. On the day of his second inaugural, a well-known evangelical pastor decided to share on Twitter his view that he was "praying for our president, who today will place his hands on a Bible he does not believe to take an oath to a God he likely does not know."[11] This was a pastor who had not even met Obama, who never responded to outreach from staff and did not reach out to the president or his staff himself. Yet he felt comfortable making a determination of the state of the president's soul and sharing it with the world.

The president—indeed every politician—is not an avatar. Our politicians are not cardboard cutouts on which we can take out our anger, exempt from even the most basic human decency. As Christians, we cannot treat a person's faith as a game, as just one more political football to throw around carelessly. A good baseline test to use is whether you would treat a member of your own congregation the same way as you do the president. Do you publicly question the faith of members of your congregation depending on their political views? Do you kick people out of your congregation depending on those views? If members of your congregation said they believed in Jesus, would you urge them on in that faith or undermine it?

Obama would come to the National Prayer Breakfast in 2011 to deliver the most extended statement on his personal faith that he has ever delivered as president. It is worth noting again here that his testimony—and this speech was very much written as a testimony—began with a paragraph about his mother, the values she taught him, and how because of her "example and guidance," and despite the absence of a formal religious upbringing, "my earliest inspirations for a life of service ended up being the faith leaders of the civil rights movement." Obama mentioned Martin Luther King Jr., a Protestant, but continued on to say "there were also Catholic leaders like Father Theodore Hesburgh, and Jewish leaders like Rabbi Abraham Joshua Heschel, Muslim leaders and Hindu leaders."[12]

He continued: "Their call to fix what was broken in our world, a call rooted in faith, is what led me just a few years out of college to sign up as a community organizer for a group of churches on the Southside of Chicago. And it was through that experience working with pastors and laypeople trying to heal the wounds of hurting neighborhoods that I came to know Jesus Christ for myself and embrace him as my lord and savior."[13]

I knew those words were in the speech, but it was special to hear the president of the United States say them out loud. The audience exploded in applause.

The president went on to describe some of the things that nourished him, including having "pastor friends like Joel Hunter and T. D. Jakes come over to the Oval Office every once in a while to pray with me and pray for the nation," receiving "consistent respite and fellowship" at the chapel at Camp David, the "meditations from Scripture" Joshua DuBois sent each morning, and even a prayer circle a family friend had started for him. This information was intended, in part, to fill in gaps in the public knowledge about his faith. Sure, he didn't attend a local church now and his former pastor was Jeremiah Wright, but now he was ministered to by two evangelicals, received a meditation in the morning from a member of his staff, and counted on prayers from folks around the country.

The weight of this evidence was then leveraged for the president to say this:

My Christian faith then has been a sustaining force for me over these last few years. All the more so, when Michelle and I hear our faith questioned from time to time, we are reminded that ultimately what matters is not what other people say about us but whether we're being true to our conscience and true to our God. "Seek first His kingdom and His righteousness and all these things will be given to you as well." [14]

This is my house, too, the president asserted once again.

Obama continued to describe "a few common themes" that recur in his prayer life. First, a desire "to help those who are struggling." He nodded to the work of faith-based charities, saying, "It also helps to know that none of us are alone in answering this call. It's being taken up each and every day by so many of you . . . so many faith groups across this great country of ours."[15]

In the weeks before the breakfast, I'd been told that the president wanted to lift up an inspiring story of a charity that was doing exceptionally good work. Months earlier, I had come across Charity: Water, founded by Scott Harrison. Charity: Water funds and supports partners around the world that provide water and sanitation services to local communities. Their work is impressive not just for what they help provide but how they respect and engage donors. The organization puts 100 percent of its online donations toward its projects, leaving overhead costs to big donors who are willing to give money to pay for things such as staff salaries and office space. They also allow donors to track the projects they fund, creating an empowering, grassroots-focused way of funding international development work that holds the promise of transforming the entire sector.[16] In fact, the US Agency for International Development has been working to implement similar improvements in its programs—respecting and empowering taxpayers and ensuring they know their money is put to good use.

"Because of Scott [Harrison]'s good work, 'Charity: Water' has helped 1.7 million people get access to clean water. And in the next 10 years, he plans to make clean water accessible to a hundred million more," the president reported. "That's the kind of promoting we need more of, and that's the kind of faith that moves mountains."[17] One of the many joys of my job was calling someone like Scott the night before a speech and telling him he might be interested in what the president had to say the following morning.

The president closed his speech with perhaps the most explicit public statement about his faith during his first term, by offering that his third prayer was that "I might walk closer with God and make that walk my first and most important task." He elaborated:

When I wake in the morning, I wait on the Lord, and I ask Him to give me the strength to do right by our country and its people. And when I go to bed at night I wait on the Lord, and I ask Him to forgive me my sins, and look after my family and the American people, and make me an instrument of His will.

I say these prayers hoping they will be answered, and I say these prayers knowing that I must work and must sacrifice and must serve to see them answered. But I also say these prayers knowing that the act of prayer itself is a source of strength. It's a reminder that our time on Earth is not just about us; that when we open ourselves to the possibility that God might have a larger purpose for our lives, there's a chance that somehow, in ways that we may never fully know, God will use us well.[18]

The president did not talk about his faith as often as some presidents, and he clearly favored bringing it up to specifically faith-based audiences and at funeral or memorial services, but it is incorrect to say that he never talked about his faith. I would often joke with other staff about the fact we could count on a new article coming up every time the president talked about his faith that discussed how rare it was. In fact, one conservative journalist, who was no Obama supporter, wrote several stories complaining about the lack of coverage of the president's faith remarks among press. She noted in one of them, "Remember how much the media covered those polls showing that huge chunks of people in all parties were confused about Obama's religion? Isn't that at least partly an indictment of how the media cover Obama's own words about his faith? Even when he speaks very clearly about his own religious views, the news is covered but not highlighted, pushed to the margins or sent out on the wire without fanfare."[19]

All this was in stark contrast to the actions of a media obsessed with other personal details regarding the president. To note just one example, he sang a line from the Al Green hit

"Let's Stay Together" and the moment was looped on cable news for days.

Part of the reason for the lack of coverage was skittishness from the White House communications team. I got the sense that some of the president's communications advisors believed engaging faith issues was more trouble than it was worth. They didn't understand faith; therefore, the reactions to the president's statements on faith were unpredictable to them. And there are few things communications staffers hate more than not being able to accurately predict what the response will be to an action or statement the president makes. When recommendations were made that would bring more attention to a faith event the president was doing, they were often rejected. I heard from one reporter who e-mailed a White House communications staffer to ask him about one of the president's speeches to a faith audience, and the staffer told him it "was not important," so the reporter didn't bother to write about it.

The president's Easter Prayer Breakfast was one of the most striking opportunities for the media to report on his faith. Each spring, in the East Room of the White House, the president delivers a gospel message to a room full of Christian leaders. I mean "gospel message" quite seriously. I remember one evangelical pastor telling me on his way out of one breakfast that the president gave "a clearer gospel message than I've heard in many churches I've visited." The message the pastor heard that morning included the following peroration:

For even after the passage of 2,000 years, we can still picture the moment in our mind's eye. The young man from Nazareth marched through Jerusalem; object of scorn and derision and abuse and torture by an empire. The agony of crucifixion amid the cries of thieves. The discovery, just three days later, that would forever alter our world—that the Son of Man was not to be found in His tomb and that Jesus Christ had risen.

We are awed by the grace He showed even to those who would have killed Him. We are thankful for the sacrifice He gave for the sins of humanity. And we glory in the promise of redemption in the resurrection.

And such a promise is one of life's great blessings, because, as I am continually learning, we are, each of us, imperfect. Each of us errs—by accident or by design. Each of us falls short of how we ought to live. And selfishness and pride are vices that afflict us all.

It's not easy to purge these afflictions, to achieve redemption. But as Christians, we believe that redemption can be delivered—by faith in Jesus Christ. And the possibility of redemption can make straight the crookedness of a character; make whole the incompleteness of a soul. Redemption makes life, however fleeting here on Earth, resound with eternal hope.[20]

I walked into my first Easter Prayer Breakfast with two evangelical leaders. As they scanned the room, we discussed how refreshing it was to see so many Christian leaders gathered in the same room. Every year at the breakfast you could have a Catholic bishop, an internationally known evangelical pastor, a head of an African American denomination, a leader of a Christian social service agency, and a Christian music artist—all at the same table! But I also remember the regret that struck my two friends when they realized how many of the people in the room they did not know personally. It should concern Christians that it requires a presidential invitation to bring them together.

These breakfasts contained a host of memorable scenes: the president's joy at seeing the children's choirs perform; the sermons that were delivered and the encouragement and urging on the messenger received from his or her fellow clergy; the times of prayer that hushed us, just for a moment, and provided the burdened leaders refuge. Most memorable of all, perhaps, was a moving performance by Sara Groves.

Sara is an award-winning singer-songwriter best known for her song "He's Always Been Faithful to Me," a modernizing of the classic hymn "Great Is Thy Faithfulness." I'd contacted Sara and asked if she would perform "He's Always Been Faithful to Me" at the 2012 breakfast.

When Sara began playing, the room immediately knew the hymn her song invoked, so when she finished the final chorus, she turned to face the audience and said, "I wonder if you would join with me in singing." As Sara struck the opening chords of "Great Is Thy Faithfulness," a pressure valve was released. Suddenly, clergy—black, white, and brown; progressive and conservative; young and old—were back in the churches of their childhood, not in the White House. Folks who didn't know one another an hour ago were grabbing onto shoulders, encouraging one another with the truth of the hymn's promise. And all around the room, clergy and cabinet secretaries and social service workers and the president began singing "Great Is Thy Faithfulness." The power of the moment was palpable. (I believe this moment was in the president's mind as he considered singing "Amazing Grace" in his eulogy to Rev. Clementa Pinckney, one of the victims of the Charleston, South Carolina, church massacre.)

The president has talked about walking around the White House sometimes late at night. He'll walk through the hallways and think about the decisions presidents have had to make. About the decisions he has to make. I can't help but think of the president walking through the East Room at night, not to mention the staff who pass through every day. That room was sanctified the morning Sara led us in worship, I think. And I believe the songs of praise that rose that morning must still echo through the walls of the White House even today. That melody of God's faithfulness is now as much a part of the history of that room as Nixon's farewell speech or the mourners that passed through it to pay Lincoln his final respects. I think God makes use of that type of thing.

2012: FAITH AND POLITICAL VIEWPOINTS

In his first three prayer breakfast speeches, President Obama covered the intersection of faith and his administration, faith and public life, and faith and his personal life. To round out his first four speeches, he would return to his 2006 address and touch back on the theme of faith and politics or public policy.

Because Obama was no longer one of a hundred senators, the remarks would carry new weight. He was now the head of the American government, and the demographic changes in the country regarding the rising population of nonbelievers and the religiously unaffiliated were becoming evident.

It is important to understand that 2012 was the first of two years where the keynote speaker was antagonistic toward the president. After the president's deeply personal speech in 2011 was followed by several policy moves and statements that many in the faith community, particularly evangelicals, believed to be egregious, my sense is that a decision was made that it was not tenable to offer the president a forum to speak to the religious community uncontested, so to speak. Thus in 2012, Eric Metaxas was the keynote speaker. Eric is an evangelical who lives in New York City, holds a degree from Yale, and has a cutting, sophisticated wit. His speech was slyly confrontational and winsome, and it was his presentation of contestable statements paired with his air of sophisticated humor that, I believe, got under the president's skin. Metaxas also sought to preempt the personal religious rhetoric of the president's last prayer breakfast speech by repeatedly referring to the difference between talking the talk and walking the walk. However, the force of Metaxas's approach was blunted because the president's speech this year was entirely about how his beliefs influenced his actions.

The president littered his remarks with several ad-libbed digs. For the third year in a row, he included (this time in his opening) a recognition of how prayer allows us to slow down amid the busyness of daily life. The section was originally drafted to close with "We can all benefit from turning to our Creator, listening to Him." But the president added, with an insistent tone, "avoiding phony religiosity, listening to Him."[21]

The meat of the speech began after a recap of some of the religious evidences that he'd described more in depth the previous year. "But I don't stop there. I'd be remiss if I stopped there, if my values were limited to personal moments of prayer or private conversations with pastors or friends. So instead, I must try—imperfectly, but I must try—to make sure those values motivate me as one leader of this great nation."[22]

The president then launched into a section of the speech that was probably as annoying to political conservatives as Ben Carson's talk would be the following year to political liberals. He walked down a list of major issues and accomplishments from his first term and tied them back to explicitly religious values. So his efforts to rein in financial institutions and prevent insurance companies from discriminating against Americans were not just because he "genuinely believe[d] it will make the economy stronger for everybody," but because "I believe in God's command to 'love thy neighbor as thyself'"—a call, he would say, was found "in every major religion and every set of beliefs." His talk of shared responsibility was not just because of his understanding of civic duty and the responsibility of privilege, but it also "coincides with Jesus' teaching that 'for unto whom much is given, much shall be required.'" On opportunity: "I am my brother's keeper." On foreign aid: "the biblical call to care for the least of these" and to "answer the responsibility we're given in Proverbs to 'speak up for those who cannot speak for themselves, for the rights of all who are destitute.'"[23]

These values are "old," he said, and can be found among "many denominations and many faiths, among many believers and among many non-believers." They are "values that have always made this country great," he said, before another ad-lib: "when we live up to them; when we don't just give lip service to them; when we don't just talk about them one day a year."[24]

The point of this section of the speech, which I worked on closely with staff, was not to argue the president had a monopoly on figuring out how values translate into policy. Instead, it was to assert that his values drove his positions on many issues; to not cede a conversation about values, and even after a difficult year with the faith community, remind them of shared ground.

The next two paragraphs seek to make this clear:

> Now, we can earnestly seek to see these values lived out in our politics and our policies, and we can earnestly disagree on the best way to achieve these values. In the words of C. S. Lewis, "Christianity has not, and does not profess to have, a detailed political program. It is meant for all men at all times, and the particular program which suited one place or time would not suit another."
>
> Our goal should not be to declare our policies as biblical. It is God who is infallible, not us. Michelle reminds me of this often. So instead, it is our hope that people of goodwill can pursue their values and common ground and the common good as best they know how, with respect for each other.[25]

It was great to check off my bucket list "work on speech with the president of the United States in which he quotes C. S. Lewis." These two paragraphs represented core aspects of my political theology—a perspective that I saw in Barack Obama from 2004 and that I am glad he gave voice to, a perspective that sought to disentangle Christianity from a set of mere political viewpoints. Yes, we seek to have our faith infuse our politics as we do all areas of our life, but we never confuse the infused with the Infuser. The middlemen—you and me!—are too imperfect for that.

The president closed his speech with a recounting of his recent meeting with Billy Graham. President Obama was the first sitting president to visit Billy Graham at his home, and the president recounted how after Graham prayed, "I felt the urge to pray for him."

The president would conclude: "I have fallen on my knees with great regularity since that moment—asking God for guidance not just in my personal life and my Christian walk, but in the life of this nation and in the values that hold us together and keep us strong. I know that He will guide us. He always has, and He always will. And I pray His richest blessings on each of you in the days ahead."[26]

I would leave the White House in May 2012 to lead faith outreach for the president's reelection campaign. The four prayer breakfast speeches the president gave while I worked there provide a comprehensive picture of his approach to faith during his time in office. And that approach is worth careful consideration, for our response to it reveals much about our own views regarding the intersection of faith and politics.

The tension Americans face when listening to their elected leaders is neither to ignore the fact that politicians have political goals, nor to disregard the reality that politicians are human beings with convictions, doubts, and hang-ups like all of us. As Americans, and particularly as Christians, we get into trouble when we excuse the bad from our favored leaders as simply "the cost of politics," while simultaneously dismissing as without value the actions or words of our typical political opponents. Rather, we ought to affirm what we find to be good and reject what we find to be bad, regardless of its source. Our politics would benefit from people who are willing to take such steps.

THE PRESIDENT'S LEGACY

Historians will consider the president's legacy for decades, and the actions of his successors will have a significant impact on how his presidency is viewed by history. We know that Obama entered office during a time of profound challenge for America at home and around the world. His administration brought America back from the brink of the Great Recession and saved the auto industry. Unemployment would be about half of what it was when he began his first term. And, of course, he will certainly be remembered for the Affordable Care Act and the millions of Americans who gained access to health care. Indeed, it is possible that Barack Obama will join the company of Franklin Delano Roosevelt and Lyndon Johnson, progressive reformers who enacted enduring sweeping policy changes that became integral to the American social safety net.

Obama has also changed the politics of foreign policy during his tenure. He has significantly raised the bar for the justification on the use of ground troops. In diplomatic efforts to countries such as Iran and Cuba, he has potentially opened up a new era of American engagement. He doggedly insisted on international cooperation and obligations when it was politically inconvenient for him to do so, including his administration's support for international aid to help feed and heal those in need around the world. In the area of foreign policy, Obama has, in general, governed as he campaigned. Of course, Obama's approach to foreign policy will be judged in large part by what happens in nations such as Iran, Israel, Cuba, Syria, Iraq, and Afghanistan in the years to come. And while history may judge his hesitancy to more drastically intervene in Syria as a steely, principled decision to avoid another intractable commitment in the Middle East, the human cost of that choice, and the loss of a generation of Syrians either killed or uprooted from their homes, will likely cast a shadow over the president's foreign policy record when it is recorded by historians. What is certain is that as a matter of both domestic national security politics and the global balance of power, Obama's presidency has been deeply consequential.

The president's legacy will also be shaped by the inherently historical nature of his presidency as the first black president of the United States, and the message that has sent to Americans and the rest of the world. Racial injustice and racial tensions became central issues during the president's second term. I hope and pray we will look back and see that it was during Obama's time in office when issues that festered out of the sight of many were brought into the light so that we might deal with them, as a nation, and move toward healing.

The grace, compassion, brilliance, and dignity with which President Obama served will transcend any partisan historical judgments. His basic, apparent decency was more consequential because he was the first black president, but it will set a new benchmark that will apply to all future presidents regardless of their backgrounds or ethnicities.

There was a photo in the hallway leading into the Oval Office that was there early in the president's first term through my entire time in the White House. While other photos were rotated out, this one remained. It showed the president in the Oval Office, bending over at practically a ninety-degree angle, while a small African American boy placed his hand on Obama's head. The boy had asked if the president's hair really felt like his, and so Barack Obama bent down and told him to check it out for himself. Before

Obama, at no other point in our history would a boy like him have ever thought to ask that question.[27]

Barack Obama understood early on the cultural power his election and presidency would wield. It would seem impossible to measure the impact of this particular power, but perhaps not. Perhaps we will look back in several decades and realize this was the beginning of a new diversification of the talent pool for policymakers and elected officials. Or the beginning of a resurgence of marriage, fatherhood, and family life. The cultural power of politics, and of Barack Obama specifically, should not be underestimated.

But there is one final legacy issue that must be discussed, and this is the promise of Barack Obama to push back against polarization, to turn the page on the culture wars, and to bring bipartisanship back to American politics. On this central aspiration of his 2008 campaign, he unquestionably failed. The president admitted his regret on this count in his final State of the Union address in 2016. A media and campaign finance system that incentivize polarization and, as we have already discussed, Republican intransigence played a role, but it should be clear that President Obama and his administration made concrete policy and political decisions that directly fueled partisanship, polarization, and the culture wars.

Each of the following five chapters covers a particular season of controversy or conflict, and the ways in which the presentation of issues, the structural realities of our media and political institutions, and the strategies of politicians and strategists conspired to drive polarization to the truly corrosive levels we see today.

CHAPTER 6

SEARCHING FOR COMMON GROUND ON ABORTION

The issue of abortion has roiled American politics for decades because the issue raises potent political ideas and values: life, liberty, privacy, autonomy, and power. It brings to mind inherently personal questions: Who deserves a future? How far into our personal lives should the values and ethics of our community reach? For many people, abortion makes us think of our families, and of the family members who were or were not born. We think of our own existence, and whether there is inherent value in that alone. At what point did I matter? At what point did you?

Abortion has played a role in our politics for more concretely partisan reasons too. For decades a significant percentage of Americans were "single issue voters," casting their vote depending on the candidate's position on abortion alone. Abortion has also become integral to identity politics as it is often suggested that all women are pro-choice and all Christians are pro-life.

This leaves little room for individual thought and, of course, the inconvenient demographic of Christian women.

Abortion and reproductive issues have been influential in modern presidential elections, though the ideological alignment on the issue has shifted. As historian Daniel K. Williams observed, men used to support abortion rights more than women, and abortion rights were once opposed by Democrats and civil rights groups and supported by libertarian-inspired Republicans.[1] It was Ronald Reagan, who was formerly pro-choice, who became president in large part because of his stated opposition to abortion and the support from evangelicals he received in return. After twelve years of Republican control of the White House, and the solidification of the modern left-right divide on abortion, Bill Clinton ran in 1992 by moderating the tone of his party's strident pro-choice stance and committing to make abortion "safe, legal, and rare." George W. Bush followed Clinton in 2000 with a promise to restore a culture of life in America. In 2004, John Kerry, a Catholic, repeatedly tripped over the issue of abortion, and the archbishop of Kansas City promised during the campaign he would deny Kerry communion if he attended church in his diocese due to his pro-choice views. The issue remains one of the most reliably divisive in American politics today.

LATE-NIGHT E-MAIL

Barack Obama recognized this and understood any vision of unifying the country could only be taken seriously if it addressed the issue of abortion. He took the issue head-on in his book *The Audacity of Hope.* In it, he tells of an e-mail he received in the wake of his victory in the 2004 Democratic primary for the US Senate seat he would eventually win. Dr. Farr Curlin opened his e-mail by congratulating Obama on his primary victory and indicating he was considering voting for Obama in the general election. However, Curlin was surprised by the rhetoric on Obama's campaign website regarding abortion, rhetoric that "you," referring to Obama, "of all people, certainly know obscures the reason for the deeply contentious nature of the abortion debate." Curlin pressed in, writing to Obama, "Your website parrots the old saws" about right-wing ideologues who want to "take away women's rights." Then he pleaded with Obama, "as a man who will likely exercise enormous power on behalf of others (I believe you will win and may go on to be President one day), please leave behind the obscurantist and ad hominem rhetoric that currently characterizes your website's approach to this issue."[2]

Curlin then requested Obama spell out his views on abortion and his justification for them. Would he at least agree that "abortion is a matter of killing human fetuses?" He continued, "Whatever your convictions, if you truly believe that those who oppose abortion are all 'ideologues' . . . then you, in my judgment, are not fair-minded enough nor wise enough to serve us as Senator." Curlin concluded, "Again, I don't even ask at this point that you oppose abortion, only that you speak about this issue with fair-minded words."[3]

At 1:15 a.m. the night after his primary victory, Obama wrote a reply. He was only able to "make a few quick points," but he admitted his website had "fallen victim to some of the short-hand and jargon of the Democratic party, and that is not always a healthy thing. It is very difficult not to fall prey to some of that rhetoric." He then went on to acknowledge abortion is a "profoundly difficult question," but he believed "it should be the woman, and not others, that acts as the final decision-maker."[4]

The doctor's earnest e-mail might have been part of the motivation for Obama to make comments during the 2008 campaign that concerned portions of his pro-choice base. He told a reporter for *Christianity Today* that he was open to certain restrictions on abortion.[5] He advanced the idea that there were common ground policies that would reduce abortion without interfering with a woman's right to choose.

Even in 2008, this did not lead to a "kumbaya moment" with the pro-life movement. Right-wing groups declared that Obama would be the "most pro-abortion president" in history.[6] The primary basis for this claim was a speech Obama gave to Planned Parenthood stating his support for the Freedom of Choice Act, a sweeping bill the pro-choice lobby was pushing that would basically overrule state restrictions on abortion. Though he was clearly on the left, some worried Obama was backing away from his support for the bill.[7] His votes in the Illinois state senate were consistently in line with the positions of the most ardent pro-choice advocacy organizations.[8]

NOTRE DAME

This history of abortion politics, national and personal, made what the president did five months into his first term—near the height of his political capital—both surprising and risky. Obama went to Notre Dame University to try to build a bridge.

The run-up to the commencement address was tense. I had the sense that many members of the president's staff viewed the effort as futile at best, and a solicitation of distraction and division at worst. There was some merit to their concerns. Notre Dame's decision to grant Obama an honorary degree (a conventional thing to do for any commencement speaker) was met with criticism and protest from conservative Catholics and pro-life activists. Some called for the president of the university to resign.

Rather than give an easier, predictable speech on an issue where there was more traditional agreement between Democrats and Catholic institutions, Obama decided to address the potential for common ground on abortion.

Rhetorically, Democrats had long been for making abortion "rare," but it was typically just that: rhetoric. Barack Obama was different. The fact that he was giving the speech at all proved it. The way he stuck his neck out on the issue during the Democratic primary proved it. He would show again that he was willing to take risks to build a bridge.

After hours of deliberation, the draft of the speech staff had prepared included the new Democratic compromise language that had been agreed upon for the 2008 Democratic platform: Democrats support "reducing the need for abortion." It took significant back-and-forth negotiations to agree to this language. It was a compromise because pro-choice activists didn't want to give up the rhetorical ground of affirming abortions should be "reduced," while the language forces pro-life advocates to concede that abortion is "necessary."

The president rejected this contrived approach. His speech was on abortion reduction, and he was going to say that. On the way to South Bend in Air Force One, the president replaced the compromise language with "reduce the number of women seeking abortions." This was not compromise; it was common ground, and he was going to stand on it.

There were protests on the day of the commencement speech,

but Notre Dame president John Jenkins's efforts and communication of the university's values helped to reduce tension leading up to the speech. Still, during the president's introductory remarks, protesters yelled, "Abortion is murder! Stop killing children!" Much of the rest of the audience responded with chants of "We are ND!" and "Yes, we can!" The president then said something striking: "We're fine, everybody. . . . We're not going to shy away from things that are uncomfortable sometimes."[9]

After a recitation of the major challenges our nation faced—war, economic crisis, and looming environmental catastrophe—he added another generational challenge: "We must find a way to reconcile our ever-shrinking world with its ever-growing diversity—diversity of thought, diversity of culture, and diversity of belief."[10] Without this reconciliation, we would be unable to confront the challenges that affect us all, he told the graduates.

He then told the crowd the story of Dr. Curlin, returning to the moment when he stepped back from demonizing the other side, and prayed "that I might extend the same presumption of good faith to others that the doctor had extended to me." He continued, "because when we do that . . . we discover at least the possibility of common ground."[11] The president was asking pro-life Americans to give him a chance.

MAKING GOOD ON THE PROMISE

Before the speech at Notre Dame—following the mandate the president gave to the faith-based office as described earlier in this book—a senior-level policy process was already established to carry out the president's vision. The promise of that speech was slowly smothered over the course of more than two years of staff work.

I was a part of a small team of staff that included Melody Barnes, the president's domestic policy director; Tina Tchen, who was then the head of the Office of Public Engagement and a longtime women's rights leader; and Joshua DuBois, the head of the Office of Faith-Based and Neighborhood Partnerships. Other policy staff rotated in and out as the process and job transitions required, but Melody, Tina, Joshua, and I were a part of the effort for its duration.

I enjoyed and looked forward to these meetings, particularly because of the people involved. I adored Melody Barnes, head of the Domestic Policy Council. Her portfolio included the faith-based office, so I worked with her frequently. Barnes was simply one of the most compelling people I served with in government. Her brilliance was unqualified. She was a strong, humble leader. She had an almost regal presence and an unreserved laugh. As the leader of the Center for American Progress's Faith and Progressive Policy Initiative, Barnes also had an understanding of dynamics in the faith community that many others lacked. I learned a great deal from working with her.

I met Tina Tchen in Iowa during the president's campaign. She was a volunteer who had brought her daughter to share in the experience, and I fell in with her, as I did not yet know anyone on the campaign, and she had a welcoming presence. I did not know that Tchen was a supremely accomplished lawyer in Chicago, nor did I know that she would end up as the president's first director of the Office of Public Engagement, only leaving that role to serve as the First Lady's chief of staff. She had a gregarious disposition, and her team seemed to enjoy working with her. I did. As an adoptive mother, Tchen came through time and time again to support the president's work on adoption.

I had the privilege to work with many incredible, accomplished, and effective women early in my career. They did their work with little of the bravado or frat house showmanship that characterizes the work of many men in politics. Melissa Nitti, Liz Allen, Marie Harf, Darienne Page, Sonal Shah, Lauren Dunn, Allison Zelman, Elizabeth Wilkins, Martha Coven, Jamie Smith, Leah Katz-Hernandez, Jenny Urizar, Stacy Koo, Stephanie Valencia Ramirez, Danielle Gray, Danielle Boorin, Marta Urquilla, Evan Maureen Ryan—they all served as role models who exemplified that while "politics ain't beanbag" as the old saying goes, you don't have to lose your humanity to get ahead. Of course, there were also male staffers who exemplified this as well—Denis McDonough chief among them. In the long run, few want to work with a bully, not to mention be led by one.

Over the course of the initiative to "reduce the need for abortion,"[12] we met with more than a hundred leaders and advocacy groups, held dozens of internal meetings, and spent hundreds of hours on draft documents. The end goal was clear: create a set of common-ground policies and administrative actions that move our politics beyond the zero-sum game of the culture wars, and actually reduce abortion by addressing its root causes.

Our work was focused on identifying policies in five buckets: preventing unintended pregnancies, supporting maternal and child health, opening up pathways of opportunity for women and mothers, promoting healthy relationships, and strengthening adoption. There was ample common ground available, and we made great progress in defining it: strengthening enforcement to prevent pregnancy discrimination in employment, combating sexual coercion in relationships, improving access to information regarding prenatal care, and supporting innovative partnerships between adoption service providers and women's health providers. I have no doubt that with the White House's focused leadership, and a willingness to spend political capital on the effort, the president's vision could have been realized.

But zero-sum politics won. Pro-life groups, most of which might as well be legally incorporated into the Republican Party, did not want to give a pro-choice president the victory of leading the charge to reduce abortions. Moreover, they had already warned the country that the president would be the "most pro-abortion president in history," thus making it difficult to partner with him.

One of our early outreach meetings was with a conservative women's pro-life group that staunchly opposed the president in the 2008 campaign. I was proud we were meeting with them. The president committed to listening to all Americans, and this was a concrete way he was keeping that promise. The meeting was cordial—at least from our side. In the run-up to the meeting, the organization's leader went on a media tour hyping up the meeting. This was highly unusual—organizations do not typically publicize private outreach meetings with the White House—and it drew attention and criticism from some quarters that suggested we should not have met with the group in the first place.

The meeting itself went smoothly: it was a listening meeting on our part, so our primary goal was to hear their perspective and see if there was any proposal we might be able to consider.

At the end of the meeting, the organization's leader asked if she could pray for us. The prayer was essentially that God would change the president's mind on the issue of abortion. The meeting wrapped up, and within hours the prayer was public knowledge. To me, generating self-serving publicity around a meeting intended to explore ways to reduce abortion was a cheap ploy. These types of antics on the Right worked to confirm the doubts of our friends on the Left.

The White House and progressive allies weren't always constructive either. After eight years of President Bush, who opposed abortion and spoke about a "culture of life," pro-choice activists (and policymakers) were looking to advance their views on women's rights; they decidedly did not want to use political capital on an initiative that ceded an inch of rhetorical or policy ground. The ideology, the skepticism, and the defensiveness of progressives, even some of the president's own staffers, were a roadblock. In one meeting we received a memo back from the Oval Office that included a note from the president asking about an abstinence-only program that had been reported on the front page of the *New York Times* earlier that week. The program was evaluated to be promising, and the president had made a commitment to consider all programs— even abstinence-only programs—that proved to be effective. I was proud and in awe to see this memo with the president's note in the margin, visible proof once again of his earnestness in seeking common ground. He at least wanted to run the story to ground to see if the program was legitimate. But when the note came up in a meeting, eyes rolled, and one staffer even commented with a sigh, "Does he read everything?" Usually, this comment would be in unreserved admiration, since we Democrats prided ourselves on caring about the latest research and "evidence-based policies." But in this case, it sounded more like a complaint. In 2016, some progressives celebrated the Obama administration zeroing out the budget for abstinence-only education programs.[13]

The president's desire to consider policy options without ideological blinders on was a problem in other areas too. There are two ways to put together a common-ground proposal: First, you can only include lowest-common-denominator policies—policies all of the major players agree on wholeheartedly. Second, you can put together a package that makes both sides uncomfortable, but achieves enough that each side is willing to agree to something it considers less than ideal. Unfortunately, opposition to policies supported by the pro-life community—opposition sometimes grounded in real policy concerns, others in cultural or ideological reaction—would prevent these policies from receiving full consideration.

By the end of 2011, hopes of following through on the president's commitment were virtually slashed. Any trust that existed between sincere pro-life actors and the White House had eroded due to our unwillingness to take taxpayer funding of abortion off the table as a part of the Affordable Care Act. We knew the bill would not pass without doing so, but in order to delay disappointing women's groups, the White House waited until the pressure built to the extent that pro-life Democratic members made public promises to vote against the ACA. The president ultimately signed an executive order addressing abortion in health care reform, but the damage was done. We had strained relationships with faith-based allies who did not understand why we did not take funding for abortion off the table at the outset, and Democrats sacrificed over a dozen pro-life Democrats in the mid-term elections. This gutting of pro-life Democrats in the House, as well as the big Republican victory overall, made it even less likely we would be able to move forward with the common-ground effort. By the end of 2011, the contraception mandate controversy (discussed in the next chapter) was in full swing, and our work was swamped by that tide.

Finally, the Department of Health and Human Services denied the United States Conference of Catholic Bishops (USCCB) a grant to serve trafficking victims solely because USCCB would not perform abortions. This decision was made even though USCCB scored highest in evaluations as the country's most effective service provider and even though they had previously received the grant. The president was not happy about the process that led to the decision, but it was clear evidence that his temperament and judgment on these types of issues did not filter down to his staff.[14]

By the time of the president's reelection campaign, Democrats were running against the Republican "war on women." In his second term, he opposed a ban on abortion after twenty weeks. The ban, the White House suggested, threatened the health of women.[15] In the president's entire time in office, the White House did not propose one restriction on abortion, even though the president stated he was "completely supportive of a ban on late-term abortions" in the final presidential debate in 2008.[16] He repeated his openness to restrictions on abortion throughout the 2008 campaign. That he never took any action to propose or actively support such a restriction as president suggests that either those statements were little more than political posturing, or his intentions were overwhelmed by political calculation and compromises once he was president. Pressed on all sides, the president's grand vision from Notre Dame was overwhelmed by culture war politics.

BOTH SIDES FAIL US

The issue of abortion is not going anywhere anytime soon. Advancements in our understanding of biology, of human life, have reinvigorated a conversation for a new generation—one that is skeptical of those with power trampling upon the vulnerable— about what a commitment to justice demands when it comes to abortion. When pro-choice advocates try to paper over or misdirect attention from these factors, they only exacerbate the public's discomfort with abortion. Outside of DC, Americans on both sides of the abortion debate know it's more complicated than the simplistic narrative pro-choice advocates often offer.

Similarly, pro-life Americans should acknowledge that abortion is contested precisely because it is morally fraught, with rational and even compassionate arguments on both sides. And while most of us generally have the luxury of holding to dogmatic lines without the responsibility of implementation, policymakers do not have that option. Pro-life Americans—pro-life Christians, in particular—should not ignore the consequences of their ethics because they do not foresee that they themselves will have to bear those consequences.

Importantly, although the president never did have that magic moment of breakthrough on abortion—imagine, for instance, a press conference where he was joined by the head of Planned Parenthood and prominent pro-life religious leaders to announce a robust policy package to reduce abortions—the fact of the matter is that by the end of his second term, the abortion rate in this country was the lowest it has ever been since *Roe v. Wade*.[17] Many of the policies that were under consideration as part of the common ground effort were enacted, albeit for a variety of reasons.

ADOPTION: A BRIGHT SPOT

One of the key areas of progress was with adoption. I had the privilege of helping to lead the White House's work on adoption and foster care in partnership with staff at the Department of Health and Human Services. My interest in adoption policy was not only rooted in my personal passion for the issue but because general support for adoption was a promising area of common ground between the political parties. I worked closely with a range of outside stakeholders to make progress, including Nicole Dobbins of Voice for Adoption, Chuck Johnson of the National Council for Adoption, and Rita Soronen with the Dave Thomas Foundation for Adoption. But there was no outside expert more central to my work on adoption than Kathleen Strottman, the executive director of the Congressional Coalition on Adoption Institute (CCAI). Kathleen served as a close aide to Senator Mary Landrieu for years before taking leadership of CCAI. Senator Landrieu was the undisputed champion for adoption in the US Senate for years until she lost her seat in 2014. The CCAI's principal function was as a nonpartisan resource on adoption and foster care policy to members of Congress. Kathleen became my most trusted outside advisor on adoption issues. She also became a true friend, a rarity in Washington.

The Obama administration, in partnership with state governments, advocates, service providers, faith-based organizations, and others, made important progress on adoption during my time at the White House. A significant factor was rising awareness in the faith community of domestic foster-care adoptions. Evangelical leaders began speaking up about the fact that in our own backyard, tens of thousands of foster kids were legally separated from their parents and waiting for adoption. If they aged out of the foster-care system, their odds of unintended pregnancy, dropping out of high school and not attending college, involvement in the criminal justice system, and many other negative outcomes skyrocketed.[18] Those who age out are also more likely to become victims of human trafficking or forced prostitution.[19] Despite this, much of the evangelical conversation around adoption focused on international adoption.

Working across various agencies, the administration and its partners worked to improve outcomes for kids in foster care and promote foster-care adoption where possible. During National Adoption Month in November, I had the honor of planning events to celebrate adoption. Two years in a row, Health and Human Services (HHS) secretary Kathleen Sebelius personally participated in these events, which culminated with her presiding over the adoption of foster-care youth from populations that were statistically less likely to be adopted.

In 2010, one of those adoptions was of Thomas McRae. Thomas was abandoned by his birth mother when he was one month old and left with a man dying of colon cancer. Because of his illness, the man put Thomas in the homes of acquaintances, eleven different homes. When he was ten years old, he was accidentally shot by the grandson of his current caretaker, and child services placed him in foster care. In foster care, he was diagnosed with PTSD as a result of getting shot. In the sixth grade, he developed a friendship with a classmate, Dawson, whose mother, Joi Morris, suspected Thomas was in the foster-care system. Joi began to take adoption classes as the boys' friendship developed. One night, after Thomas's twenty-second home and eleventh foster-care placement, Thomas called Morris on the phone and asked, "Will you adopt me?" She did. Finally, Thomas had a forever home. We were able to commemorate that adoption in a ceremony, as Thomas stood in front of Secretary Sebelius with his mother and his new brother, his friend Dawson, as Sebelius cried while trying to read the ceremonial language.

Two and a half years later, the *Washington Post* published a profile of Thomas.[20] He was an intern for Senator Ben Cardin. He briefed an entire committee of members of Congress on his experience in the foster care system, and his policy suggestions to improve it. At the time of the profile, he was in college pursuing a BA in psychology. He was voted Mr. Freshman and Mr. Sophomore his first two years in college, served as his dorm's head resident advisor, and was developing his talent as a poet. He loves, and is loved by, his family.

When I arrived at the White House in 2008, there were 463,792 children in foster care and 79,392 children legally separated from their parents and waiting for adoption. When I left in 2012, there were 397,122 children in the system, and 58,625 waiting for adoption.[21] This progress was the result of efforts by state and local governments, advocates and adoption agencies, as well as the federal Administration for Children and Families—and it was an honor to support this progress from the White House, to shine a spotlight on it and assist where we could. That assistance included multiple years of staff work in support of making the Adoption Tax Credit permanent, which the president signed into law in January 2013. The adoption tax credit helps families cover the costs—which can be expensive—of pursuing adoptions. It makes adoption possible for thousands of families who would otherwise never consider it.

In 2011, I organized the Obama administration's first National Adoption Month event at the White House. The event was streamed live online and attended by advocates, policymakers, and religious leaders from across the country. I was most proud of the day's final panel. The topic was domestic foster-care adoption and featured both David Wing-Kovarik, an LGBT adoption advocate, and Kelly Rosati, a vice president at Focus on the Family who oversaw their pro-life and adoption and orphan care programs. Because of the participation of cabinet-level officials, and the fact the event would be streamed live, I was concerned that at some point in the planning process questions would be raised about including a speaker from Focus on the Family. Somehow, that never happened.

Kelly was an important person to have on the panel. Kelly oversaw Focus on the Family's Wait No More program, and it was a revelation. In partnership with Colorado's governor, a Democrat, Wait No More engaged dozens of congregations to recruit adoptive parents for waiting children in foster care. Though Kelly is always sure to share credit with the adoption agencies and other ministry efforts in Colorado, Wait No More was central in the dramatic reduction in the number of kids in Colorado foster care waiting for adoptive families. Where once there were more than 800 kids, the number shrank to approximately 250. Since Colorado, Wait No More has worked in 20 states and more than three thousand new families have begun the process of foster care adoption across the United States.

Due to their religious convictions, the Wait No More program did not recruit LGBT adoptive parents, nor did it support cohabiting couples adopting. Yet even though their perspective on some issues differed from that of the Obama administration, their work still deserved to be lifted up. Their contribution was still valuable. So they appeared on the panel alongside someone (Wing-Kovarik) who vehemently disagreed with their policy, where it was explored respectfully. Instead of running from or ignoring differences, they were confronted, and the best of both perspectives was celebrated. With the 2012 election less than a year out, that was a coup, indeed.

In addition to progress on adoption, other important policies that fell in the common ground "buckets" also advanced. Senator Bob Casey's Pregnant Women Support Act, which provided important supports for maternal health, was included in the Affordable Care Act and signed into law. The Equal Employment Opportunity Commission (EEOC) stepped up enforcement of pregnancy discrimination cases. The Earned Income Tax Credit and Child Tax Credit, bipartisan tax policies that help support low-income families, were expanded.

Again, one would think that those who believe abortion is the taking of an innocent life would be the loudest people celebrating these accomplishments. But politics too often gets in the way of applauding what is good. Pro-life Americans should ask why prominent pro-life groups decided to target pro-life Democrats rather than focusing their efforts on pro-choice politicians in both parties. The Democratic Party has moved to the left on abortion in recent years for many reasons, including political calculations and ideological consolidation, and the Obama administration has unfortunately provided justification for pro-life groups' skepticism. In 2014, a government report found that the administration has failed to enforce, or not even tried to enforce, the rules regarding federal funding for abortion.[22] The pro-life Democrats in Congress lost their seats defending what turned out to be a lie—that the president's commitment that health care reform would not result in federal funding for abortion. In this case, the Obama administration proved the cynics right. In 2016 the Democratic Party took an unprecedented, extreme position on abortion by calling for a repeal of the Hyde Amendment in their party platform. This made support for taxpayer funding of abortion party dogma.

As important as it was to enact key policies like the adoption tax credit, and as promising as it is that the abortion rate has fallen, I cannot help but think about what could have been if the Notre Dame vision had become reality. Imagine if after forty years of intractable, tit-for-tat politics, our political and cultural leaders had managed to join hands to take concrete action together. Imagine if this issue that divides us so powerfully had been transcended by shared purpose. I often wonder what it will take to get there.

CHAPTER 7

THE CONTRACEPTION MANDATE

"What should we do on contraception?" someone asked.

I was in one of our group's small, intimate meetings, working to reduce the need for abortion. The focus of this meeting was on the prevention plank of the agenda, a vital section of our report for the president's political base—but addressing it was tricky. Previous iterations of Democratic attempts to reduce abortion in Congress had amounted to little more than using the rhetoric of abortion reduction as a Trojan horse for massive increases to Title X family planning programs. Moreover, in order to maintain the effort as common ground, we knew that the more we did to support contraception, the higher the bar would be to pull in pro-life actors, particularly Catholics, who held a doctrinal opposition to contraception.

Another staffer weighed in, with a tone full of delicate meaning, to suggest that we postpone the conversation on contraception, as health reform would likely address the issue.

The staffer was referring to a provision in the Affordable Care Act that mandated health insurance coverage for preventive services but deferred determining what services would be included to a separate process led by the Institute of Medicine (IOM). While advocates, lawmakers, and other policymakers expected this provision to cover contraception, the fact that this was not explicitly outlined in the legislation helped avoid a controversy that would have further complicated the bill's passage. The staffer suggested we table the topic of contraception until the IOM made its decision.

This was the first time several of us had heard about this provision and what it was expected to accomplish. The air in the room thickened with the implications as we processed this information, and the rest of the meeting was an absolute blur. It was clear to me that significant decision makers did not understand how profoundly burdensome this would be for many religious organizations.

WHAT'S THE BIG DEAL, ANYWAY?

Early on, the *New York Times* reported on the possibility that contraception would be covered by the ACA. Administration officials quoted anonymously said they "expected" the recommended services from IOM to include contraception and family planning, but "the officials said they preferred to have the panel of independent experts make the initial recommendations so the public would see them as based on science, not politics."[1] The report noted that the inclusion of birth control as a mandated service was "likely to reignite debate over the federal role in health care," and that it was already "raising objections from the Roman Catholic Church."[2]

The conflict here for many religious groups was twofold. First, because our health insurance system is employer based, the IOM recommendation—if accepted by HHS—would mean every employer that provided its employees with health care would also be required to provide their employees coverage that included contraception. For most Protestant Christians, contraception that prevents fertilization—condoms, for instance—does not run counter to the teaching of their faith, though some Protestants have begun to revisit the matter. But for Catholics, contraception in all forms runs counter to their sexual ethic—contraception is, as a matter of doctrine, immoral. Moreover, the IOM recommendation also covered emergency contraception that some consider "abortive," though this is a matter of debate.[3] Whatever the state of the science, opposition to emergency contraception is widely held among Catholics and evangelicals.

The second problem for some religious groups was that the contraception mandate amounted to the government's endorsement of a utilitarian, demoralized sexual ethic. They feared the government's definition of contraception as a routine, mandated "preventive service" would send a powerful message to society that separated sex from marriage and procreation, and treated sex as simply a recreational activity that required risk management. And to be sure, many have argued for years for just that kind of national consensus. Expanded access to contraception was central to fulfilling that goal.

In July 2011, the Institute of Medicine recommended that contraception—including the morning-after pill—should be included as a preventive service under the ACA—along with mammograms and various kinds of screenings and immunizations. Secretary Sebelius called the report "historic," and added that "these recommendations are based on science and existing literature."[4] Per the 2010 Affordable Care Act, the Health and Human Services secretary would make a final determination on what services would be included in the "preventive services provision" that insurers must cover free of charge. The next month, Sebelius and the Department of Health and Human Services announced an initial draft rule that would require virtually all religious employers to pay for health insurance that included contraception. The rule included a religious exemption, but the definition used to define *religious* was narrow—much more narrow than the IRS definition—and basically covered houses of worship. Most religiously affiliated hospitals, colleges, religious orders, social service organizations, and religious businesses, such as Christian bookstores, would not receive an exemption. The mandate would go into effect on August 1, 2012.

The White House had been in discussions internally and with outside groups for months, long before the initial ruling came out. In these internal discussions, we wanted to ensure everyone understood the stakes, especially the ramifications of forcing religious employers to cover contraception in their health insurance plans. I became convinced early on that there were legitimate constitutional issues at play, as well, and I worked to make clear we had to consider the potential for legal, not just political, challenges if we didn't get the policy right. On some occasions, legal concerns were dismissed out of hand.

With outside groups, we assessed the range of positions on the mandate and then sought to communicate those views in a way that could be understood in the West Wing. Some religious groups and leaders utterly opposed the mandate, while some completely supported it. Other religious leaders would support the mandate so long as it had a robust religious exemption—with, of course, various interpretations about what qualified as "robust." And then there was another contingent that was opposed to the mandate but would "hold their fire" and not publicly mobilize against the administration if there was an exemption. This is just a sampling of the perspectives we heard on the issue.

It was clear the Catholic bishops conference and some evangelical groups would oppose the mandate, even if it included the broadest religious exemption that could reasonably be considered. Their opposition would not surprise anyone in the White House, though the extent of their opposition could range from a press release to an unprecedented national campaign. It was also clear that without a robust religious exemption, centrist and even some liberal religious advocacy organizations would be against the mandate and would mobilize against it. This is what elevated the issue beyond a standard disagreement between conservative religious advocates and a progressive White House, but instead a potentially landscape-shifting, conflict-stoking move. This reality was conveyed to the highest levels of the White House repeatedly.

As negotiations proceeded, moderate religious groups largely held their fire as they met with White House and HHS officials, in the hopes that they would prove themselves to be good-faith actors not interested in scoring political points, but in getting a fair policy outcome.

The entire four months between the initial rule in August and the announcement of the final rule was intense, but things really picked up in November. That month, Vice President Biden arranged for Cardinal Timothy Dolan of New York, the head of the US Conference of Catholic Bishops, to meet with President Obama. Along with the faith-based office, Biden and the president's chief of staff, Bill Daley, argued internally for a stronger exemption than what was in the initial rule.

According to reports, the president personally expressed regret to the cardinal over how the HHS grant to serve trafficking victims (discussed in chapter 6) was handled, and he was deeply engaged in the discussion with Dolan about the bishops' concerns with the contraception mandate.[5] Afterward, Dolan expressed in private and in public that he was encouraged.

The meeting was a shock to the system of those internally and externally who opposed a broader exemption. According to one account, "The Dolan meeting sent nervous jitters through pro-choice and women's groups who were pushing to keep the interim rule. They intensified their lobbying, relying on White House senior advisor Valerie Jarrett and Kathleen Sebelius, secretary of Health and Human Services, as their main allies."[6] The *New York Times* similarly reported that "Cecile Richards, president of Planned Parenthood, and other proponents of the rule began a series of meetings with officials to argue against an exemption for religiously affiliated institutions."[7]

In December 2011, HHS overruled an FDA recommendation to make emergency contraception available over the counter to minors. As pro-choice women's groups strongly supported the FDA recommendation, their dismay was leveraged to build pressure around the idea that the administration should not decide against women's groups for a second time.[8]

Additionally, an electoral argument was made. A senior political advisor reportedly thought "the bishops' complaints could bolster a useful campaign narrative: that supporters of their view, including Republican Mitt Romney, held anachronistic views about women and family planning."[9]

At the White House, those of us who were uncomfortable with the initial rule pushed for a solution that would maximize women's access to free contraception while respecting the conscience rights of religious organizations, particularly nonprofits and obviously religious employers, such as religious book publishers. Melissa Rogers, who would become the head of the faith-based office in the president's second term, proposed in the *Washington Post* a federal solution based on a Hawaii law that effectively placed the burden for contraceptive coverage on the insurer, not the employer.[10] The president's chief lawyer insisted such a workaround, really any workaround, was not possible.[11]

We also tried to break through the shallow analysis that suggested all the president's political allies were on one side of the issue. The clearest example of this was Sister Carol Keehan, one of the loveliest people you could ever meet. The president of Catholic Health Association (CHA), Sister Keehan essentially oversees all Catholic hospitals across the country. She cares passionately for the poor and those without access to health care, and it was this passion that led her to support the Affordable Care Act over the opposition of the American leadership of her church. The president gave out twenty-one pens when he signed the Affordable Care Act into law; twenty of them went to policy staff and members of Congress. Only one advocate received a pen: Sister Carol Keehan. The Affordable Care Act simply would not have passed without her.

Therefore, one would think her concern about how the ACA contraception mandate affected her hospitals—and religious freedom—would gain a hearing. And she did gain a hearing. The president's top health care policy advisor in the White House, the person who led the charge on the Affordable Care Act, consistently raised Sister Keehan's concerns. The president spoke with Sister Keehan directly. It was not enough.

THE WRONG DECISION

I received the news late one January afternoon: there would be no change to the initial rule, not even a nod toward compromise or change after months of outreach, and religious organizations would have a year to comply. The narrow religious exemption would stand. This was a unique moment: never had one single policy question taken up so much of my time, for such a long time, making it all the more devastating when the wrong decision was made. In the announcement about the decision, Secretary Sebelius said the rule "strikes the appropriate balance between respecting religious freedom and increasing access to important preventive services."[12] She added that "scientists have abundant evidence that birth control has significant health benefits for women,"[13] emphasizing the strategic tactic of senior political staff to convince the public the decision was "based on science, not politics" that was reported in the *New York Times* almost a year earlier.[14]

The outcry should not have surprised anyone in the White House. The Catholic bishops committed to educate and mobilize their parishes, and Cardinal Dolan claimed the decision proved the president misled him in their Oval Office meeting. Religious Right groups had a field day.

Then there were those who generally supported the administration. Seven of the current members of the president's own faith council wrote to him about their concerns with the mandate. The president of Notre Dame, who had stuck his neck out for the president in 2009, came out against the policy. E. J. Dionne, the progressive Catholic columnist for the *Washington Post*, whom the president reads often, wrote a scathing column that argued the president failed to live up to the commitment of his 2006 Call to Renewal address. Dionne said that the "administration mishandled this decision not once but twice. In the process, Obama threw his progressive Catholic allies under the bus and strengthened the hand of those inside the church who had originally sought to derail the health care law."[15]

Typically pro-choice newspaper editorial boards wrote against the policy. The daily press briefing on some days was dominated by questions from the press about the policy. Senator Bob Casey, who was one of the president's earliest endorsers in 2008, publicly opposed the president on the rule. Leaders of Catholics for Obama, who had supported the president's election and would be counted on again in 2012, wrote a letter of their own. Scot McKnight,[16] Jim Daly,[17] and other evangelical leaders were sounding alarm bells. Jewish leaders were speaking out to voice concerns the administration was setting precedent with its novel definition of what counts as a religious organization. It was a mess.

In an e-mail to some senior staff, I summarized the fallout from the decision, pointing out that this was one of the few core issues that unified different denominations and those of various political leanings: "the ability of the Church to thrive while remaining true to its core beliefs—religious liberty."

I went on to summarize the actions even relatively apolitical Christian leaders were taking to protest the mandate. I included an e-mail from one religious leader who noted he was progressive politically, but that the administration's decision to keep the initial rule was one of those issues that would make it very easy to vote for another person. He added that there were a lot of people who felt the same way.

There were signs early on that the president was open to changing the policy. Even on the day the decision was made, Obama expressed to Sister Keehan in a phone call that future changes were possible before the mandate was put into effect.[18] A few days later, Obama was "as angry as his senior aides had ever seen him."[19] The *Los Angeles Times* reported: "Now, the president was telling his aides that he had read the legal opinions and policy papers on the issue, and he saw no reason why a more accommodating solution had been ruled out."[20] "Fix this," the president ordered his staff.

On February 7, David Axelrod went on MSNBC's "Morning Joe," and indicated another change was coming, saying, "We certainly don't want to abridge anyone's religious freedoms, so we're going to look for a way to move forward that both provides women with the preventative care that they need and respects the prerogatives of religious institutions."[21]

On February 10, the president went to the daily briefing to announce that the policy would be changed so that "if a woman's employer is a charity or a hospital that has a religious objection to providing contraceptive services as part of their health plan, the insurance company—not the hospital, not the charity—will be required to reach out and offer the woman contraceptive care free of charge, without co-pays and without hassles." He insisted that under the new rule, "women will still have access to free preventive care that includes contraceptive services—no matter where they work."[22]

The announcement alleviated the political pressure in the short term. As the *New York Times* reported, the change was "never really driven by a desire to mollify the Roman Catholic bishops . . . rather, the fight was for Sister Carol Keehan."[23] Keehan and the leaders of other major Catholic organizations such as Catholic Charities, Sisters of Mercy of the Americas, and the Leadership Conference of Women Religious responded favorably to the February 10 announcement. The president of the Association of Jesuit Colleges and Universities reported that he was "really appreciative of what the president did last Friday. I'm optimistic and hopeful, and I feel the religious liberty issue is addressed."[24]

I do not know how the bishops would have reacted had the policy described by the president on February 10 been what was announced on January 20. But following the release of the "final" rule on January 20, the bishops had their backs up against a wall. Conservatives within the bishops' conference had been strengthened, using the initial rule as proof the Obama administration could not be trusted. Although Cardinal Dolan initially told the president the policy change was a "step in the right direction," by the end of the day the bishops were warning the plan raised "grave moral concern."[25]

The bishops launched a full-scale campaign called the Fortnight for Freedom, which included rallies across the country and an intensive education campaign. The campaign made a difference: Catholics across the country were more educated and concerned about the state of religious freedom as a result of the Fortnight for Freedom effort. In my view, the bishops' staff did harm their effort by suggesting a religious exemption in the mandate should include virtually any employer who had a religious objection, regardless of the type of work—including a Taco Bell franchise. This position—what one writer called a "striking overreach by a formidable foe"[26]—overshadowed more reasonable objections and aided those who sought to make any critiques of the mandate seem extreme and out of touch.

Despite the president's statement that the issue was not a "political football," it became a centerpiece of the effort to reelect him. In May, Planned Parenthood's political action committee launched an unprecedented $1.4 million ad campaign that argued Mitt Romney wanted to "deny women the birth control and cancer screenings they depend on."[27] The Democratic Party argued explicitly that Romney was part of a war on women. The Obama campaign ran an ad in which a woman said, "I've never felt this way before, but it's a scary time to be a woman," and then a narrator described Romney's opposition to the mandate simply as a total opposition to "requiring insurance coverage for contraception."[28] This was all part of the strategy to "bolster a useful campaign narrative."[29]

In June 2012, after months of negotiations on the specifics of the plan the president announced on February 10, Sister Keehan announced that she would, in fact, not be able to support the proposed accommodation. In response to an "Advanced Notice of Proposed Rulemaking," Keehan wrote a five-page letter detailing why CHA would be unable to support the rule, urging the administration to change its position to protect the freedoms of religious organizations and to ensure the CHA would be able to continue its work serving the vulnerable. Liberal Catholic writer Michael Sean Winters wrote that the letter required that "everyone who is morally serious . . . take notice."[30]

Over the next three years, the mandate would be adjusted at least eight times, with each adjustment promised to be the one that found the right balance. Thus on June 28, 2013, the *National Catholic Reporter* headline read "Obama administration issues final rules on HHS contraceptive mandate."[31] The *Wall Street Journal*'s headline on August 22, 2014, was "Administration Offers Contraception Compromise for Religious Employers."[32] And on July 10, 2015, *The Hill* headline declared "Feds Set Final Rules for Birth Control Mandate."[33]

The mandate brought the administration into direct, unnecessary conflict with organizations that serve the most vulnerable people and provide invaluable service to this nation, and therefore it misdirected attention and resources from serving people to legal fees and public relations battles. Despite the numerous adjustments, many religious organizations, including the US Conference of Catholic Bishops, still oppose the mandate. In July 2013, CHA announced its concerns were adequately addressed after another round of adjustments.[34]

The contraception mandate has been the subject of dozens of lawsuits from evangelical and Catholic institutions, and businesses and nonprofits owned or run by religious people. Though the Supreme Court upheld other aspects of the Affordable Care Act twice, it ultimately ruled against the contraception mandate in *Burwell v. Hobby Lobby*. In 2016, a case initiated by the Little Sisters of the Poor reached the Supreme Court. Here, the Court took the unusual and, for the administration, humiliating step of playing mediator by ordering supplemental briefs that basically asked both parties (the Little Sisters and the federal government) whether there was a reasonable arrangement that could be made that would allow women to get contraception coverage and the Little Sisters' consciences to be respected. The Court understood these were not habited Machiavellis, but women with sincere religious claims and consciences that deserve protection, if possible. The first paragraph of the Little Sisters of the Poor brief contained their answer to the question of whether they thought their consciences could be protected while their employees received contraception coverage—yes. After almost fourteen pages of "hemming and hawing," in the words of Stanford law professor Michael McConnell, the federal government said yes too.[35] In an interview after the Supreme Court's ruling in the Little Sisters case, President Obama said the ruling meant that "women will still be able to get contraception," and "we are properly accommodating religious organizations that have objections to contraception."[36]

What all of this means is that the administration could have better accommodated religious organizations at the outset, in August 2011, without hindering their policy goal of expanding women's access to free contraception. They just chose not to do so. They chose the path of most resistance.

A July 2014 profile of Vice President Joe Biden by Evan Osnos contained several curious lines. Osnos noted that the vice president objected to the initial rule of the contraception mandate and, without citing any specific individuals, reported that "some of Obama's political advisers concluded that Biden's political radar was out of date."[37] But Biden's political radar was not out of date. The initial rule, the rule Biden opposed, had to be revised more than eight times. It was rejected by the Supreme Court. It spawned a sustained attack accusing the administration of initiating a war on religion. It divided Americans. Joe Biden's political radar is just fine. If the mandate was not a political problem, why did the president order his staff, probably including the "political advisers" who made judgments about Biden's political radar, to fix it?

RELIGIOUS FREEDOM AND THE OBAMA ADMINISTRATION

The controversy was bad for America, and it was bad for religious freedom. This is not just because of the contraception mandate itself but because of what the resulting fight did to the idea of religious freedom in this country: it made religious freedom a partisan idea.

I do not believe that anyone I worked with in the Obama administration, certainly not the president, was motivated by a desire to undermine religious freedom. That was not their aim. Religious freedom is not under attack.

But it is under pressure. Religious freedom is increasingly butting up against other values in stark, personal ways, and religious freedom is often the loser in those collisions. We have a problem of pluralism, of different views and perspectives. What must be declared out-of-bounds is not our diverse perspectives, but the kind of zero-sum politics that disregards collateral damage in pursuit of a win. And the administration failed in this respect.

The Obama administration's record on domestic religious freedom and inclusion is not all negative. The president has rejected calls to refuse government grants to organizations that organize and hire around religion. The administration defended the National Day of Prayer in federal court and won. The EEOC fought workplace discrimination based on religion. The administration successfully defended in the Supreme Court a Muslim woman's right to wear religious clothing in her retail job. The president spoke out forcefully on behalf of religious minorities' rights to be free from discrimination and fully included in American life.

But there were serious missteps as well. The HHS mandate is the most profound, but there were others. The administration advanced an argument in the Supreme Court case *Hosanna v. Tabor* that completely denied, over objections from some in the White House, a ministerial exemption under the free exercise and establishment clauses. The case involved the question of whether a Lutheran school could make hiring decisions in line with their religious doctrine. The legal argument brought forth by the federal government drew shock during oral arguments not just from the conservative justices but also from Justice Elena Kagan—the president's own appointee, and his former solicitor general. All nine Supreme Court justices, including the president's two appointees, decided in favor of the Lutheran school and reaffirmed the legal doctrine of a ministerial exception that is more than forty years old.

There is also a culture of fear and anxiety around the future of religious freedom that the president has mostly chosen to ignore. These concerns are legitimate and spurred by real cases. In New York City, a misguided interpretation of the separation of church and state led to a multiyear controversy in which churches using public school buildings for services on Sunday were under threat of being displaced. On college campuses around the nation

Christian student groups have been derecognized because they require their leadership to be Christian. In Houston, pastors had their e-mails and sermons subpoenaed to see if they had advocated against a government policy objective. The Supreme Court decision that legalized same-sex marriage warned of unresolved religious freedom questions, and in the arguments for that case, the solicitor general left the door open to drastic restrictions on religious freedom. The president has been virtually silent on all of these issues and has offered little public comment on his broad view of religious freedom in light of the legal, social, and political developments of the twenty-first century.

Even as the contraception rule was adjusted to be more reasonable, the debate over it struck at several central premises of the president's campaign. The struggle over this mandate reinforced concerns about an activist government that the president has spent his entire time in office trying to alleviate. I believe an active government, particularly in the service of the vulnerable, need not come at the expense of constitutional freedoms. I think that is a false choice. But those who disagree can point to this mandate as evidence for their position.

It also reinforced the idea that religious people cannot trust Democrats, suggesting that the promise of the president's religious outreach was just an insincere political tactic.

We don't know what those two men at the airport think now, but a reporter, Greg Jaffe, actually followed up with the doctor from Chicago, Dr. Curlin. Curlin, Jaffe reported, had thought the president seemed to understand the "totalizing nature of Christian discipleship," and the "profound importance" of religious freedom. But it was the president's handling of the contraception mandate that led him to question his earlier assumptions about Obama's understanding of religious freedom. Curlin told Jaffe that eight years after Obama's election, religious people feel less free to live out their faith, particularly when those teachings run counter to "modern mores."

Jaffe explained: "Curlin doesn't blame Obama for that broader societal change, but he thinks his decisions have contributed to it. 'Insofar as he's had policies come up that might either arrest that trend or accelerate it,' Curlin said, 'he has chosen unquestionably to accelerate it.'"[38]

CHAPTER 8

THE PRESIDENT'S "EVOLUTION"

In the winter of 2008, on the suburban streets of Bettendorf, Iowa, I met my first "project" voter. She was a middle-aged woman who opened up the door only slightly when I knocked. I learned that she was a Christian and a lifelong Democrat. She thought Republican economic philosophy left out the middle class. She liked Barack Obama, in particular, but she could not vote for a candidate who supported gay marriage, and she did not believe the Democrats, including Barack Obama, when they said they opposed it.

Most campaign staffers would not have thought she was worth our efforts, but these were exactly the kinds of voters I felt I could reach. I believed she was mistaken. She was one of the countless Americans fooled by the talk show radio hosts and figures on the divisive Religious Right who called the president a liar. On the campaign, accusations the president supported gay marriage were turned around to suggest the extremism of those making the claim. *Don't these people have any obligation to the clear, reported truth?*

I wrote this voter a letter, quoting the president's words and his official policy stance on gay marriage, and I assured her that the president could be trusted. I'd heard him state his position clearly myself, and I believed him.

THE PRESIDENT'S OPPOSITION TO GAY MARRIAGE AND HIS ELECTION VICTORY

The president's opposition to gay marriage was crucial in 2008, not just with moderate and conservative white voters, but with the African American base that propelled him to victory over Hillary Clinton. Through the fall of 2007, Clinton was leading Obama among black voters. Obama had lost his first congressional race by being dismissed as an Ivy Leaguer who wasn't really from the community that his opponent, former Black Panther Bobby Rush, represented. The same might have happened with black voters in primary states had he supported what was at the time considered an elitist position.

The gospel concert events in South Carolina that laid the groundwork for his crucial victory in that state would have been much more difficult to pull off if he had a formal position in support of gay marriage. In fact, the issue became relevant around these events. Donnie McClurkin, a headliner for one of the events and an award-winning gospel singer, describes himself as "delivered" from same-sex attraction. This had been known for some time, but a liberal blog began criticizing Obama for "sucking up to bigots" and providing a platform for McClurkin.[1] I was not on the campaign at the time, but I later learned that people very high up in the campaign wanted McClurkin uninvited, but in the end he was not. Why? African American voters would have seen it as a betrayal.

Instead, an LGBT minister was invited to participate in the event as well, and the controversy was turned into one other example of Obama bringing people together and making sure all had a seat at the table.

To me, Obama's stance on LGBT issues was just another way he was going to turn the page on the culture wars. He was deeply passionate about basic LGBT rights and made them central to his campaign. It seemed to me that these rights—hospital visitation, employment and workplace protection, repealing "don't ask, don't tell," and others—could be supported by Christians. Gay people shouldn't have to die alone in a hospital bed because their partners weren't allowed to visit. No biblical tenet requires that. To think of those who died alone—from AIDS, from cancer, from ailments that find us all—should make us shudder.

Prominent evangelicals had done important work rooted in their theology on these issues. Rick Warren helped lead evangelicals from justifying AIDS to fighting it, and it was two evangelicals in the White House, George W. Bush and his aide Michael Gerson, who mobilized the power of the federal government to combat global AIDS. At some cost, evangelicals such as Joel Hunter, David Gushee, and others of national stature advocated for basic LGBT rights in areas such as employment.[2]

Yet for more than two thousand years, while there have been different approaches to marriage among Judeo-Christian traditions, what has been unanimous within the disparate visions is that marriage is a gendered institution. In the Christian faith, marriage is not merely a contract, but explicitly, mysteriously, a reflection of the very relationship that we have with our God. It is taken quite seriously.

Fewer than three months from Election Day, Obama sat across the stage from Rick Warren and indicated he took it seriously too. Senator Obama answered Warren's request to give a definition of marriage by saying, "I believe that marriage is the union between a man and a woman. Now, for me as a Christian it's also a sacred union. You know, God's in the mix."[3]

It is, in fact, hard to overstate the number of times the president in public and private, in meetings with clergy and others, affirmed his opposition to gay marriage. In his 2004 Senate debate with Alan Keyes (who, as discussed earlier, had put Obama on the defensive regarding his religious beliefs), Obama agreed without caveat that marriage is not a civil right.[4] In *The Audacity of Hope* he wrote: "I believe that American society can choose to carve out a special place for the union of a man and a woman as the unit of child rearing most common to every culture."[5] Just days before the election, on MTV of all places, he stated his position forthrightly and clearly: "I believe marriage is between a man and a woman. I am not in favor of gay marriage."[6]

Huffington Post published an article documenting sixteen times that Obama and his staff denied support for same-sex marriage, beginning in 1998 and continuing through to June 2011.[7]

PROGRESS ON LGBT RIGHTS

It was the president's stated opposition to gay marriage that gave him the space early in his administration, often with the support of those who did not support gay marriage, to advance LGBT rights. In his first year, the president launched an anti-bullying initiative that focused much of its attention on LGBT youth. In 2010, the president repealed "don't ask, don't tell," allowing LGBT Americans to serve openly in the military. His administration protected LGBT federal employees, combated hate crimes, and ensured hospital visitation rights for LGBT couples. I supported and worked on all of these policies. Many evangelicals and other Christians supported these policies as well. Obama seemed to show a way forward: to hold on to theological truths while respecting human dignity in a pluralistic society and protecting the basic rights of our neighbors regardless of their backgrounds or personal identities.

THE EVOLUTION

While all this occurred, some strategists aligned with the reelection campaign were preparing for a change in position, something I deduced in the winter of 2011 when I was told that according to internal polling, young people considered same-sex marriage the civil rights issue of our time.

The Department of Justice's position statement to the Supreme Court for the *Windsor* case, which eventually declared the Defense of Marriage Act unconstitutional, only bolstered this conviction. I argued that the brief removed any possible grounds for opposing the legalization of same-sex marriage. If this was true, I wanted to know, as it would be the responsibility of the faith-based office to develop a plan that was as sensitive as possible to the friendly and supportive religious leaders who had been told repeatedly the president's position was firm. I at least wanted a longer runway so the news would not be sprung on folks.

That is not how it worked out. On May 6, 2012, Vice President Biden announced his support for same-sex marriage on *Meet the Press*, which moved up the timeline for the president to announce he had changed his mind as well. Later reports indicated the president had decided months earlier that he would announce his support for same-sex marriage in the weeks leading up to the Democratic convention to avoid an intraparty fight over how the platform should address the issue.[8]

On May 9, Obama sat down with Robin Roberts in a hastily prepared interview to make the historic announcement. His statement contained in it years of preparation and thinking about the issue and, therefore, was quite dense and had many distinct elements. First, the president completed the story of his evolution, which was now clearly meant as a sort of narrative device, and indicated his evolution had led him to this point.

Next, the president argued that his previous position in support of civil unions for same-sex couples was not enough. He had supported civil unions, he told Roberts, because he was sensitive to the fact that marriage "for a lot of people . . . evokes very powerful traditions, religious beliefs, and so forth."[9]

Why did he change his position on the issue? "Over the course of several years," he said, he talked to friends, family, neighbors,[10] and staff who are "incredibly committed, in monogamous relationships, same-sex relationships, who are raising kids together," and gay members of the armed services who are "out there fighting on my behalf." "At a certain point," he continued, "I've just concluded that—for me personally, it is important for me to go ahead and affirm that—I think same-sex couples should be able to get married."[11]

He went on to explain that part of the reason for his "hesitance on this" was due to his belief that marriage was a state issue, and that "this is an issue that is going to be worked out at the local level."[12]

Obama announced his support for gay marriage not by simply invoking a changed perspective on the constitution or a new insight into LGBT people's experiences, but by invoking his faith and what he thought was at "the root" of Christianity. When Roberts asked the president about whether he discussed his change in opinion with the First Lady, he responded, "You know, we're both practicing Christians. And obviously this position may be considered to put us at odds with the views of others. But, you know, when we think about our faith, the thing, you know, at root that we think about is not only—Christ sacrificing himself on our behalf—but it's also the golden rule, you know? Treat others the way you'd want to be treated."[13]

What is important to understand is that the language Obama used regarding the golden rule echoes language that was poll-tested and promoted by LGBT-rights groups as effective.[14] The initial reason he gave in the interview for reversing his position—personal encounters with LGBT people—is often cited by LGBT groups as the reason for the fast pace of change in Americans' views on the topic.

Finally, the president also said some important words about those he no longer agreed with on the subject of marriage, as he emphasized that change on this issue would happen at the local level and urged for conversation on the issue to "continue in a respectful way." He said many of those who oppose gay marriage "are not coming at it from a mean-spirited perspective. They're coming at it because they care about families. And—they—they have a different understanding, in terms of—you know, what the word "marriage" should mean. And I—a bunch of 'em are friends of mine—you know, pastors and—you know, people who—I deeply respect."[15]

Although his rhetoric on the campaign trail started out more nuanced, his campaign soon began casting those who held the same position he had just months ago as "straight out of the 1950s" and Mitt Romney as a character out of *Mad Men*, a show that features an adulterous, twice-divorced protagonist.

The president deserves respect for announcing he had changed his mind before the election, therefore giving citizens a chance to consider it as they cast their votes. But after the election he would alter his view that change should happen at the state level. His multiple references to gay marriage in major moments such as his speech at Selma and multiple State of the Union addresses also seemed to run counter to the intended impression of his promise that he would not "be spending most of my time talking about this." In 2012, voters elected a president who supported same-sex marriage, but believed it was a secondary issue and one to be determined by the states. In his second term, the president's Justice Department would argue same-sex marriage is a constitutional right, and the White House would be lit up like a rainbow. Nevertheless, in the election the people had a choice, and because of his announcement, voters had a more complete set of facts before them to help them make that choice.

The idea that some campaign aides have promoted in retrospect—in order to accentuate the political courage of the president—that it was basically a coin flip whether his change would help or hurt politically simply is not true. While some risk was involved, most believed the change had a great upside that played directly into the campaign's overall strategy of turning out its core supporters. Almost immediately, the campaign promoted the president's support for same-sex marriage and used it to draw a distinction with Mitt Romney. His position featured heavily in the Democratic convention as part of an overall narrative about Republicans being stuck in the past.[16] In the actual election results, the position change had no discernible effect on black voter turnout or allegiance, and the president won the Catholic vote nationally for the second time. His national numbers among white evangelicals matched Kerry's in 2004.

Campaign staff no longer had to deal with the personal and social tension of working for a candidate who was "not there yet," and many now acted as though he'd never opposed same-sex marriage in the first place. I remember one interview I had with the *Boston Globe* during the reelection campaign in which the reporter restated benignly the president's change from being against gay marriage to his current position, when a campaign press aide interrupted the reporter to correct him: "I don't know that I would agree with that characterization," the aide said. The reporter and I were both befuddled. *How else would you characterize the president's position before announcing he had changed his mind? What do you think he had changed his mind from?*

FULL DISCLOSURE

In the run-up to the decision and in the months after, I asked myself whether this was the plan all along, particularly as the legalization of same-sex marriage became regularly included as a signature aspect of the president's legacy. In 2015, the question appeared to have been answered in David Axelrod's memoir of his time in politics. In his insightful, alternatively inspiring and grounded book, Axelrod wrote that the president personally supported gay marriage as early as 2007, but believed it was not politically feasible to express this view. "Opposition to gay marriage was particularly strong in the black church," Axelrod wrote, "and as [Obama] ran for higher office, he grudgingly accepted the counsel of more pragmatic folks like me, and modified his position to support civil unions rather than marriage, which he would term a 'sacred union.' After one public event where he expressed his opposition to same-sex marriage, he told Axelrod, "I'm just not very good at bull——ing."[17]

This sort of thing is expected in our politics, but this instance was not just a matter of ethanol subsidies or some other relatively obscure, wonky policy issue—after all, "God is in the mix." Moreover, the president had not expressed his opposition or his support solely in terms of policy analysis or legalistic inquiry. I was forced to ask myself, *Would he really have used religious language to convince voters of something he did not believe?*

Typically, when the president is accused by anyone of lying or misleading the public, the White House press secretary vehemently denies it. That is the job of the press secretary. But when asked about Axelrod's claim after the book's release, the press secretary replied that "the president's record on these issues speaks to this even better than I possibly could."[18] In other words, the White House and the president himself were at least comfortable with giving journalists and the American people the impression that Axelrod's claim was true.

The White House's bet is clear: when the dust settles and history is written, Obama will look more like Lincoln—someone who was willing to do what was necessary for greater freedom and equality—than other presidents who have been maligned for misleading the public for their own personal ends or policy goals.[19] In an interview that day, Obama suggested David was "mixing up his personal feelings with my position on the issue,"[20] but this is, as Axelrod agreed in an interview with CNN's Jake Tapper, the very point he was making in his book—that the president had one position he told voters, and a different position in private. Axelrod explained the president's misrepresentation to the public as "not uncommon in history, great leaders often work in that way . . . he had a goal and he worked his way to that goal."[21] The White House is betting that the cynicism and political expediency will be mostly forgotten by future generations, and instead Obama will be seen as an activist president, shrewdly moving to advance the cause of same-sex marriage.

This is why his most senior advisors have given Obama credit for changing opinions on same-sex marriage in the African American community, the same community that Axelrod suggested was the reason to hide the president's views on the subject in the first place.[22] It is also why the president has taken to including the legalization of same-sex marriage as part of the story of American progress, a message repeated in State of the Union addresses, as well as commencement addresses at Howard and Rutgers universities. In his 2015 State of the Union address, he lifted up the legalization of same-sex marriage as the shining example of bringing Americans together, disregarding the fact that legalization came through the courts, not through a representative body, as well as the fact that a large minority of

Americans still oppose same-sex marriage. And as one reporter pointed out on the day of the Court's decision, "While Obama said Friday that those cheering the decision must 'recognize different viewpoints' on the issue of gay marriage, he and his aides made it clear in dramatic fashion that evening which viewpoint they saw as morally just" by lighting up the White House with the colors of the rainbow.[23]

As someone who was involved in all of the major outreach efforts around the president's various policy moves on LGBT rights in his first term, I believe the administration was surprised and influenced by the lack of broad, mainstream criticism for those policies. For all of its value and importance as an issue, the anti-bullying initiative was also clearly a politically palatable way for the administration to talk about LGBT issues early on and dip its toes in the water. Subsequently, the president's repeal of "don't ask, don't tell" received little effective religious pushback. Mainstream religious leaders and organizations were far less interested in exercising political power to prevent LGBT progress than is imagined in some quarters.

The criticism that did exist mostly came from extremely right-wing, tone-deaf organizations that did little more than raise money from knee-jerk "action alerts," while driving moderate Americans to the other side. There was little direct, nonmanipulative advocacy that would provide any caution to progressives that they were in danger of appearing unreasonable to the average American.

The lack of political cost to these moves encouraged administration officials that they could take further action and that the cost of an evolution on same-sex marriage would not be too high. By the time the Department of Justice declared the Defense of Marriage Act unconstitutional, most mainstream religious groups had gone straight from disbelief to resignation. I do not mean to suggest that a lack of religious mobilization against LGBT progress is to blame for that movement. To the contrary, I want to debunk the myth that religious groups were single-mindedly obsessed with the issue. In fact, mainstream religious advocacy organizations maintained their devotion to issues of poverty alleviation, immigration reform, life and human dignity, civil rights and criminal justice reform, and so many other areas rather than focusing on just this issue.

This jump from disbelief to resignation was due in part to the fact that the battle over the HHS mandate was fought and lost by the religious groups, but there has also been a real transformation in how religious groups considered LGBT issues that has been overlooked by most: humility now plays a much greater role in the approach of religious groups and people to LGBT issues than in the past. What is the value of a legal or political victory to affirm what marriage is if the culture does not embrace that definition? What good is a law on such an issue if it does not reflect Americans' convictions? You can legislate morality—every law has moral grounds—but what does it mean if that law does not represent a moral consensus?

JUSTIFICATION

The day that Axelrod's claim was made public, Chris Hayes—a progressive and strong supporter of gay marriage—covered the issue on his MSNBC show. Hayes is also a principled idealist—something we need more of these days. So for a segment of his program, he wrestled with the implications of Axelrod's claim and the White House's nonrefutation of it.[24] He told his audience that even though the cause of gay marriage was a good one, the idea that the president misled the public should trouble all who care about our politics. "Today," Hayes said as he opened his show, "something truly rare happened: we got a look at the inner-workings of a premeditated, politically calculated, ends-justify-the-means lie. It involves candidate, and then president, Barack Obama knowingly, willfully misleading the public." Hayes continued, "What we're talking about is wholesale misdirection."[25]

Hayes posed a useful thought experiment: "Let's say there's a young conservative libertarian coming up in the kind of Ron Paul movement, and he says, 'I think we should get rid of the minimum wage, I don't believe in it philosophically.' He starts ascending to national office, understands that's not a tenable position, runs for president and says, 'Well, of course I believe in the minimum wage.' And then kind of works with libertarian activists while in office to get rid of the minimum wage in America. And then later his advisor writes a memoir and says, 'Of course he wanted to get rid of the minimum wage the whole time.' I would be angry. I would feel like that was duplicitous, that fundamentally people had been had."[26]

The effect of the thought experiment is cynicism inducing. Hayes tried to work his way to some sort of political principle, which is that the American voter, rather than listening to what candidates say, should look at the constituencies supporting that candidate. "You are electing more than a person, you are electing a coalition of folks. And that coalition of people . . . will determine the agenda of the people you put in power. And in this case, people elected the coalition of people that was on the side of gay rights."[27]

There are several problems with this approach. First, it demands an unreasonably sophisticated level of analysis from the American voter. Second, it takes the burden off politicians to tell the truth and puts it on voters to always be looking for, even expecting, to be lied to and manipulated. Third, it reinforces the notion that politics is and should be wholly owned by special interests: If a teachers union supports a candidate, that candidate could never be considered to support charter schools or merit-based pay or changes to teacher tenure. If the National Rifle Association (NRA) supports a candidate, despite what the candidate says, voters could never trust that candidate supports even a minimalistic background check policy. Fourth, it is a complete rejection of the type of politics the president spoke of when the American public elected him in 2008: one where politicians held nuanced views just like the public did and where we don't have to view everything through a red-blue, left-right prism. Fifth, and finally, the president's winning coalition in 2008 was not a gay-rights coalition. Not only did the president win a quarter of white evangelicals and over half of the Catholic vote, but Hispanics and African Americans—groups that strongly opposed gay marriage in 2008—were central to his campaign. A Democratic polling and research firm summarized the president's approach to gay marriage in 2008 in this way: "In 2008, President Obama minimized the discussion of marriage equality and his position on the issue confused voters."[28]

If the president did believe in and support same-sex marriage in 2007 or even earlier,[29] his repeated assertions that he did not were a direct rebuke of the type of politics he said was possible.

If not, then to let the claim stand that he supported gay marriage all along is to choose political gain over the integrity of the president's own words.

But the more serious issue is of a spiritual character. If we are to take seriously the president's comments in 2008 about his faith and convictions regarding marriage—what new biblical revelation came to him in those intervening years? In courting Christian voters—whose importance to his political success is evident not just in the numbers but by the very fact that he courted them—the president repeatedly invoked not just his analysis of the constitution and of policy preference on the question of marriage but his convictions about his own Christian faith. And when he announced his support for same-sex marriage, he implicated Jesus' own words about how we should treat one another, some of the most widely known teachings in the world. Surely he knew of those teachings in 2008. What about the teachings about marriage he summarized as "God is in the mix"? Where did those go? Is God no longer in the mix?

For those who are not religious, these questions may seem immaterial. "Of course God is no longer in the mix," you might say. "He never was." But this matters. Please understand that I am not suggesting that in our nation one must have a theological explanation or justification for support of any policy, including same-sex marriage. But I did not put theology on the table for this discussion. The president did. And serious civic questions exist here that reach far beyond political gamesmanship. Our republic relies on an informed citizenry, and if that citizenry can not only be openly manipulated but also then have that manipulation openly embraced and celebrated, how are we to encourage citizenship? What, then, does citizenship even mean?

This is a great challenge to hope in our politics: not the president's position on marriage, but the fact that the road he and others took to get us here was paved with as much cynicism as it was courage. And to those who are unbothered by this, I ask: how much should being on the "right side of history" excuse?

CHAPTER 9

A DIFFERENT KIND
OF CAMPAIGN

In May 2012, less than a year after Melissa and I were married, I left for Chicago once again to lead religious outreach for the president's reelection campaign. Melissa and I had discussed the chance this could happen before we got married, but that was hardly preparation for our temporary separation. As difficult as the next six months would be, we would do them together, as we always had.

I thought the opportunity was worth the sacrifice. The job was a leadership position for the reelection of a man I have great affection and respect for, and whose policies and legacy were at stake. As a result of some of the policy decisions made in the first term, I felt greater internal tension working for him in 2012 than I had in 2008, but I still thought he would be a better president than Mitt Romney, and I was proud of much that he'd accomplished in his first term. I also believed we could run a faith outreach effort that had integrity and did not seek to bully voters. So, for instance, I made a commitment that I would never suggest that Barack Obama was *the* candidate for people of faith. I wanted to put the president's record and his position on the issues in front of voters and let each decide based on his or her own convictions.

Unfortunately, while I thought I stood on solid ground regarding my perspective on the campaign, I was on less firm footing in the press. My hire was leaked before I even made it to Chicago, which started a round of press inquiry into who I was and what my hire meant for the campaign. I was not happy about the leak, but the campaign was even less happy. Some of the campaign's communications staff believed it was an intentional leak, and that I had either planned or was aware of it. Not only was I not aware of or involved in the leak, but I was upset that the news got out because it was interfering with a smooth transition to the campaign.

As the news spread, a reporter I had worked with a bit in the past called and asked for basic personal background. He asked about my religious background, and I told him that I was an evangelical and gave him the name of the church I was attending at the time. In order to convey a breadth of religious knowledge and experience, I decided to also tell him that I was raised Catholic. Big mistake. Within hours of his story going up, the part of my personal history that I thought would convey an ability to relate to various religious communities became a line of attack. The headline on a right-wing Catholic website? "Obama hires apostate Catholic to counter Catholic bishops campaign."[1] That was one press clipping I did not share with my grandmother. Melissa and I had a good laugh over it, though—politics is crazy.

A DIFFERENT KIND OF CAMPAIGN

The 2012 campaign was a departure in many ways. The 2008 campaign had been about aspiration and open doors; about the conviction that, at least rhetorically, there was not a single voter we were not going after. The 2012 campaign was a narrow, defensive one, not so much about the future, but about stoking fears that we could be taken back to a dark past by Mitt Romney and the Republicans. The internal environment of the 2008 campaign was not devoid of hard-nosed politics by any means, but at times the 2012 campaign lacked even the presentation of a higher form of politics.

The mantras in the headquarters were "50+1" and "270," meaning that all we had to do was win half of the voters plus one in enough states to get to the 270 electors necessary to carry the election. These are sensible targets to have in a campaign: the goal of a presidential campaign is to win the presidency, and so it makes great sense from an organizational standpoint to direct everyone toward what is needed to accomplish that goal. However, we now have a politics that is content with this polarization, with the idea that "50+1" is the best we can do, and really all we need to do. This makes for a dreary campaign. I know no one who enjoyed 2012.

A CHANGING NATION

The Democratic Party has undergone tremendous demographic change in the past decade. The consequences of these changes have been buffered by having Barack Obama in the White

House, but the tensions will be exposed in the post-Obama era—particularly if the party faces a string of national losses. The party has become younger, more female, more racially diverse, and more secular. In fact, the Democratic Party is now almost evenly split between white Christians, nonwhite Christians, and non-Christians (primarily atheists and religiously unaffiliated). This has an impact on our politics already. Democratic candidates will increasingly feel pressure to criticize religious ideas and groups in order to appeal to nonreligious voters.

Another effect of our secularizing country on our politics is that fewer government and political staff understand what it means to be religious. Several stories from the 2012 campaign illustrate this well.

Soon after I arrived to the campaign, I was working in coordination with the policy team on an outreach document that described the president's positions on some of the issues that matter to people of faith. The header of the second section of the fact sheet read "Economic Fairness and the Least of These." A staffer replied on the chain of senior staff with an edited version of the document that deleted "least of these." Since there was no explanation for the deletion, and since the president had used the phrase in the past, I put the phrase back in and sent the document back around. The same staffer replied with the phrase deleted with the comment "Is this a typo? It doesn't make any sense to me. Who/what are 'these'?" The staffer simply was not familiar with the phrase from one of Jesus' most well-known teachings, a phrase that the president had used many times before.

Another instance of this disconnect took place just weeks ahead of the election. I was pulled into a senior staffer's office and was told that campaign leadership was concerned about a blog post my intern had published. It turns out that after his internship at the White House, he had written for a religious website describing how he had gone to the job with bloated expectations. By the time he left, he explained, he decided the White House was "broken like any other institution," and he realized his faith had to be in God alone. An assistant to one of the campaign's most senior staffers was sent the post by a former colleague, and when they read "broken" they took it as a political indictment: "Washington is broken," "our politics is broken," and so on.

So a minor investigation was launched that led to me having to explain to very important, very busy people who had much better things to do with their time that for Christians, everything is broken. My intern's blog post was a statement of coming to terms with fundamental Christian doctrine in his own life. It was not a political attack on the man he was now trying to elect. I explained this verbally, and then, at the request of the senior staffer, in a written paragraph so that it could be shared. I did not think I would be asked on the campaign to describe Christian theology about original sin and the grace of God, but campaigns are full of surprises. My explanation must have been satisfactory, as my intern was allowed to go to Ohio to assist in faith outreach efforts there, as had been previously planned.

GETTING PROACTIVE

Despite all this, faith remained an important part of the 2012 campaign. At first, we were almost entirely on defense. In response to the HHS mandate, the Catholic Church was running an unprecedented protest against an incumbent president's policy during his reelection campaign. I knew their efforts were having an impact, because concern for religious freedom grew more among Catholics than among evangelicals. Additionally, four years of conservative attacks that largely went ignored and unanswered from the administration had taken a toll. And as noted earlier, the strategic decision that this would be a "base" election meant we were more concerned about not dampening enthusiasm among our supporters than reaching out to voters who were on the fence.

We did, however, take some important, proactive steps in the summer. The president and Mitt Romney responded to questions from the Washington National Cathedral, which provided an opportunity to reset the faith conversation. The *Christian Post* reported on the interviews, noting that Obama's responses, which I worked on, included praise for his predecessor, President Bush, as a man of faith whose beliefs influenced his decisions on immigration reform and combating AIDS. The article also summarized the two candidates' responses, reporting that "Romney's answers tended to be short, whereas Obama went more in depth with his answers."[2]

Everything changed when Mitt Romney selected Paul Ryan as his running mate. Within hours of the announcement, I e-mailed the campaign's senior leadership that the Ryan pick was a "game changer for the faith community." After a year in which the religious narrative was relatively toxic, Romney's decision to pick Ryan offered an opportunity to shift the narrative substantially.

While Paul Ryan has been more active on antipoverty efforts since 2012, at the time he was primarily known for a budget proposal that drastically cut important social safety net and antipoverty programs. It was largely due to a historic religious coalition called the Circle of Protection—a coalition that included the United States Conference of Catholic Bishops, the National Association of Evangelicals, the Salvation Army, the Sojourners, and other national religious organizations—that Ryan's budget had been defeated. With the Ryan pick, Romney now had to fully own Ryan's budget, and the religious opposition that came with it. As I wrote in the memo, Romney could have picked anyone, but he chose a running mate whose defining idea already had the opposition of religious groups from the National Association of Evangelicals to the US Conference of Catholic Bishops. Within days, the campaign announced national and state-level Catholic endorsers to show we were willing to fight for the Catholic vote in 2012.

The Democratic convention was a mixed bag. On the negative side, the convention speakers were almost comically excited about abortion. Even Democratic pundits were surprised by how virulent the pro-choice rhetoric was at the convention. Cokie Roberts called the convention "over the top in terms of abortion. . . . Every single speaker talked about abortion, and you know, at some point, you start to alienate people. Thirty percent of Democrats are pro-life."[3]

On top of that, the Republican Party—looking for a new wedge in an era when all the wedges seemed to be working against their interests—decided to drastically increase mentions of God in their party platform to ten. Before 2012, both parties' mentions of God had been below six. In 1996 and 2000, the Democratic platform had more mentions of God than the Republicans' did, and in 2004 and 2008 the Republicans only had three and two mentions, respectively. But the Republicans had an idea and laid the trap by mentioning God ten times in their

2012 platform. Unfortunately, despite a robust, new faith section in the Democratic platform, the 2012 platform had not included the one mention of the word *God* that was in the previous two platforms—which only helped the Republicans' attack. Soon enough, Mitt Romney was pledging, "I will not take God off our coins and I will not take God out of my heart."[4] The problem was only exacerbated when the convention delegates were divided on whether to add a reference to God back into the platform and appeared to some to boo the measure.

The Democratic convention did have its bright moments from a faith perspective. One of my recommendations in my e-mail to staff following the Ryan pick was to give Sister Simone Campbell a speaking slot at the convention. Sister Simone, the well-known nun from Nuns on the Bus, delivered one of the most powerful addresses of the whole convention. Her speaking slot was not an invocation or benediction but instead a forceful argument about her Catholic values, the mission of Nuns on the Bus, and her opposition to the Ryan budget. She spoke explicitly of her "pro-life stance," a noteworthy counterweight to the tone and content of other convention speakers. Catholic inclusion continued with the decision to accept Cardinal Dolan's offer to pray at the Democratic convention, as he had at the Republican convention.

Faith engagement also helped contribute to one of the defining contrasts of the campaign. A range of religious groups had partnered to request a video from each of the candidates defining what they would do as president to combat poverty. The Romney campaign had to participate because the president was going to submit a video. The videos were released on the same day in September and featured Romney commenting more on poverty in four minutes than he had the entire campaign so far. They did a great job with the video.

Unfortunately for their campaign, a video from a high-dollar, closed-door fund-raiser was leaked just days later—the infamous 47 percent video. In the recording, Romney attributes the president's electoral success to his perception that 47 percent of the electorate is "dependent on government" and "believe they are victims."[5] When you put the two videos up side by side, it looked as if Romney talked about poverty one way in front of one crowd, and in a much more negative way in private, in front of his pals. This stark contrast helped drive the 47 percent story, which was the death knell of Romney's candidacy.

BIG DATA AND THE BENEFITS OF CONFLICT

Just weeks before the election, Governor Deval Patrick of Massachusetts visited Obama campaign headquarters in Chicago. Patrick was an Obama kind of politician. Both shared advisors such as David Axelrod, and Patrick's 2006 campaign for governor included the "Yes, We Can" slogan, priming it for the president just two years later. An African American, Patrick won in a state that is overwhelmingly white and whose major city, Boston, is known for complicated ethnic and racial politics.

Patrick, like many celebrities and politicians, dropped by the office to encourage campaign staff in the final stretch. Due to his history with Obama and key staff, Patrick had the opportunity to address all of the staff, and after stirring remarks he took questions. One of the final questions he received came from someone in my department, Operation Vote. Operation

Vote was basically the constituency operation, and it had staff who focused on four major constituency groups—African American, Hispanic, women, and youth—and other "smaller" constituencies—LGBT, disability, veterans, Native Americans, faith, and others. I did not spend political capital reminding my colleagues that people of faith comprise about 70 percent of the population.

The intern asked Patrick about Operation Vote's work and what advice he would give for motivating different constituencies. Patrick paused. "I know this isn't the kind of answer you were looking for," he began. For the next several minutes he gave an impassioned talk about how—while he understood modern campaigns—he believed Democrats were at their best when they ran on a message that appealed to all Americans, rather than sending a different message to target demographics. It was a special moment. Some of the senior staff were lining the walls, looking on in appreciation, with the same kind of awareness you would get listening to the president at times—that this was a leader who was willing to cut through the silliness and triviality of our politics.

But we had a campaign to win. And we were determined to win with data. Data-driven politics is incompatible with aspirational politics. It is willing to sacrifice a broader coalition for a few bucks, a dozen hours of free airtime, and an angrier base. It is the type of politics that allows the NRA to have an outsized impact on our national debate about guns through targeted appeals that maximize their power. And it is the type of politics that leads Democrats to send specific women—women who subscribe to a particular magazine, for instance—mailings that warn Republicans will "drag women back" with anti-choice policies while telling national press that it is Republicans who are obsessed with reproductive issues.

When you're led by data alone, you can make some pretty foolhardy decisions. To take one example, the campaign to reelect the forty-fourth president of the United States decided it would be good to include profanity in its digital outreach. One e-mail included the word *damn* in the subject header.[6] I refrained from commenting on the decision to curse in official campaign e-mails because I knew enough by then to keep my powder dry on these kinds of matters. I had smarted from the responses I received to suggesting post-adoption support for birth mothers might be a possible policy area we would want to look at, or that perhaps the CDC's numbers showing more than half of eighteen-year-olds graduate without having had sex is something we should probe rather than assuming "kids will be kids."

I did not bring the issue up, that is, until I received an e-mail from a nationally known Christian leader. She liked the president, and I believed she was a supporter. She forwarded to me the campaign e-mail with "damn" in the subject line, along with a message that she would like to forward these e-mails to personal friends to encourage their support, but given their vulgarity, she obviously could not do so. I thanked her for letting me know, and I forwarded the e-mail to other staff.

Just to make this clear: a nationally known, supportive leader was telling us that she and others like her would be able to be more helpful to our campaign if we stopped sending out e-mails with vulgarity under the auspices of the reelection campaign for the sitting US president.

The response I received could have been delivered by Siri rather than a human possessing judgment and intuitive reasoning: I was informed that e-mails with profanity have an open rate higher on average than e-mails without profanity—by a matter of percentage points.

This sort of crass decision making for marginal benefit does not belong to the Democrats alone, and certainly not just to the president. It is what enables the fearmongering propaganda Christians found in their e-mail in-boxes and in direct-mail pieces warning that Christians were "under attack" or that the Obama administration was "destroying our Christian heritage." The attacks that were shocking in the last election don't raise an eyebrow in this election, so the stakes must always be raised; the threat must always be greater.

This is the reason for the war on religion versus war on women rhetoric. It is not enough for the Right to criticize the president for prioritizing contraception access in a way that pressured religious groups unnecessarily; rather, he must be engaged in a totalizing war on religion.

Yet another outreach effort during the campaign made my heart sink. Just weeks from the election, I received an e-mail seeking my opinion about a college campus outreach called "My First Time." The voter mobilization campaign would be launched with Lena Dunham, star of HBO's *Girls*, talking in a direct-to-camera ad about her "first time." The audience thinks Lena is giving details about her first time having sex until the very end of her story when—surprise!—she is revealed in fact to be talking about her first time voting for Barack Obama. I and another staffer made it very clear that this would be offensive to many people, including some students. Imagine a student who is trying to remain abstinent or whose partner is pressuring him or her to have sex, facing a campus plastered with advertisements that compare voting for the president of the United States with having sex.

We were assured that this effort was essential to the president's success, and that since it would be run by the Democratic Party rather than the campaign itself, we had deniability and thus no worries.

The campaign was launched, and precisely what I had warned would happen did happen: Fox News, conservative pundits, and others jumped on it, and it took up a news cycle. I received angry e-mails and calls from supporters. Some people were just weirded out that this came from the campaign of a father with two teenage daughters.

What I realized, though, was that this was the intent the whole time. Distract the conservatives who couldn't help their moral handwringing, get free media for running such a daring campaign with a well-known, controversial celebrity, and hopefully even draw Republicans into a conversation about female sexuality so we could run another media campaign about—you guessed it—the war on women. This was data-driven, base-rallying politics at its most dispiriting.

Politicians have always tailored their messages to reach certain kinds of voters. What is different today is that with a niche-focused news media and the tools of big data, political campaigns can privately deliver messages to individual voters that contradict messages sent to other voters. This is how two voters can go to the polls and vote for the same person for different, even opposing, reasons.

There has been much discussion of how our country has become more polarized, not less, under Obama. As the *New York Times* noted, "Mr. Obama is likely to go down in history as a rare president whose single biggest foreign policy and domestic achievements were won with no Republican votes, a stark departure from his 2008 campaign that was fueled by the promise of bridging Washington's yawning partisan divide."[7]

There is enough blame to go around, to be sure. It is clear that from the day of his inauguration, Republican leadership decided the only way to prevent the president from controlling the political process was through near-total opposition. Republicans fueled the fire of a range of conspiracy theories ranging from accusations that the president was not born in this country to accusations the president favored Muslims and even was one himself. Some Republicans reversed their support for policies such as the DREAM Act for seemingly no other reason than that President Obama now supported them. The 2016 presidential campaign only confirmed this acceleration and deepening of polarization in our politics and the electorate.

But the president's rhetoric, the standard of bringing Americans together that he set himself, required more of him. I have outlined in previous chapters occasions in which decisions were made that stoked conflict. The White House's political strategy to "look reasonable"[8] too often became more about making sure their opponents looked unreasonable. Too often the White House would not seek to marginalize the most offensive voices but prop them up. Journalist Hunter Schwarz noticed how often the president joked about those who questioned his faith or place of birth.[9] One former aide to Obama summarized the 2012 campaign's "basic message" to voters was that Mitt Romney "hates you."[10]

The failure to ease partisanship is also a result of structural issues, like an increasingly stratified, narrative-reinforcing media environment where partisans can consume news without ever having to encounter an opposing viewpoint in a fair light. The president and his aides have pointed to the media, the influence of special interests, demographic changes, and polarization among the American voters themselves as reasons for the failure.

Journalist and former Obama aide Reid Cherlin wrote that the Obama administration "managed over six years to accomplish much of what Obama promised to do, even if accomplishing it helped speed the process of partisan breakdown."[11] That is to say, at some points policy and political decisions were made that harmed the stated goal of promoting bipartisanship. In his final State of the Union, the president told Americans that harsh partisanship and divisiveness of our politics was one of his "biggest regrets."[12]

This polarization does not just harm our politics but our own communities and relationships. A 2014 study found that "party politics is becoming a litmus test for interpersonal relationships."[13] This is a serious problem for our politics and for basic social cohesion, and if we do not make intentional decisions as citizens and voters to penalize politicians—particularly those of our own party—who stoke conflict, it will only get worse.

In his memoir, former Republican congressman and President Obama's first secretary of transportation Ray LaHood reflected on the failure to break through the polarization and bipartisanship that grips our politics:

It's easy to assume that I was bound to fail, that the promise of bipartisanship was an illusion—too far out of reach for a single Republican in a Democratic Cabinet. Too formidable a challenge for a new administration facing tremendous hardships. Too risky for a young president beholden to a largely liberal constituency. Too much of a stretch for the brand of Republicanism I represented. Too overmatched by the partisan and parochial forces arrayed against bipartisanship. But openings to change the culture of politics did present themselves. We did not take the best advantage of them, however.[14]

LaHood later commented on the president himself, recalling the president's "unique and historic opportunity to change the terms and means of debate in Washington" when he first came to the White House. "His was a vision of a postpartisan world," LaHood wrote. "And he was sincere—I am not cynical enough to believe otherwise." Yet, too often there were "mistakes in judgment and political calculation that prevented cooperation between the political parties and sacrificed vision too easily for short-term gain."[15]

THE BEST OF OUR POLITICS

One moment of the 2012 campaign, however, remains a high point for me, and a reminder that our politics can create good culture, not just division and insecurity. Jena Lee Nardella is something of a wunderkind. At age twenty-two, she cofounded and served as the executive director of Blood:Water, a nonprofit that has raised more than $25 million. Blood:Water has brought water to more than a million people in Africa and provided health care for more than sixty-two thousand people in HIV-affected areas. Her influence and example have also had an outsized impact on the justice conversation in the American church.

The Democratic convention lasts three days, so as faith outreach director I had six slots to fill for the invocation and benediction each night. Cardinal Dolan had a slot, as did Rabbi David Wolpe, Reverend Gabriel Salguero, Bishop Vashti McKenzie, and Metropolitan Nicholas (Pissare) of the Greek Orthodox Church. And Jena Lee Nardella.

For an evangelical Christian, the decision to speak at the Democratic Convention cannot be taken lightly. The last thing you want to do is get involved in a controversy that could harm your ministry, either from antireligious inquiry or from a donor base upset that you would dare pray with Democrats. Jena asked for a bit of time to consider the invitation, during which she prayed and consulted with her husband and the board of her organization, who encouraged her to take the opportunity.

I smiled when I received an e-mail from a campaign staffer flagging something in Jena's prepared benediction: she included a prayer for Mitt Romney too. I assured the staffer this would be okay, and that, well, it was too late to negotiate an alternative.

Jena later told me how it felt to be standing backstage on the opening night of the Democratic convention, watching from just behind the curtain as the First Lady delivered the most impressive public address of her professional life. The stage director came up beside Jena as she watched and said, "You see how the First Lady is owning the podium, how she is just captivating the audience? Well, in just a few minutes that podium is going to be yours. Now, I'm not religious, but I believe that you have something to say that this audience needs to hear. So I want you to go out there and own that podium. I want you to speak slowly because you have something important to say."

Jena walked out, and with head bowed and eyes closed, she led a stadium full of people in praying for Barack Obama and Mitt Romney, and for our nation.

The prayer was a ray of light in a pretty depressing campaign season. Christians and others shared the video of Jena's prayer online as an example of what can happen when we hold our faith and each other's dignity as more sacred than partisan politics.

In an increasingly polarized politics and culture, this is the role Christians can play. We can take risks in the political arena to affirm that some things are more foundational than partisan politics, and when we see others do so, we can support them as they face people who do not understand. What Jena taught us that evening was that politics can be about more than winning.

It can be.

CHAPTER 10

THE TALE OF TWO INAUGURALS

By the end of 2012, I was tired, stressed, and conflicted. The president's ability to bring Americans together was uniformly dismissed, with those on the left accusing Republicans of a conspiracy to undermine the president, and those on the right accusing the president of purposefully and unnecessarily dividing Americans and deriding Republicans. I saw merit on both sides.

As we've seen, faith had played a driving role in the president's first term and was the source of much controversy. The last hurdle to the passage of the president's legacy achievement of the Affordable Care Act was a contingent of Democrats who were concerned it would fund abortions. The most extended controversy of the president's first term was the contraception mandate that resulted from the Affordable Care Act. The sizable portion of the American electorate who believed the president was a Muslim was a national story, prompting the president and his press secretary to repeatedly address the issue. Faith played a prominent role in the president's policy agenda from climate change to immigration reform. The president moved from using his personal Christian faith to explain his opposition to gay marriage to using it to complete his "evolution" on national television by appealing to the Golden Rule.

Obama won reelection. Electorally, at least, his approach to faith appeared to be validated.

Unquestionably the president's first term changed how he thought about faith, as well as about the broader themes of hope and unity. No clearer illustration of this exists than in a comparison of how the president and his staff responded to the controversy over the selection of Rick Warren to deliver his first inauguration's invocation—and the controversy over his selection of Louie Giglio for the second inaugural.

PRESIDENTIAL PLURALISM

The decision to pick Rick Warren was the president's alone. Other religious leaders were included in a list of suggestions to the president, but the president wanted to send a message. Rick Warren was his choice, despite Warren's advocacy of Proposition 8, the California referendum that banned gay marriage in the state the same day the president was elected. I was proud of the selection. The president had been clear about his opposition to Proposition 8, and so his decision to pick Rick Warren despite their disagreement on key issues seemed to be another fulfillment of his promise to bring America together. *We can disagree on important issues,* the president's selection said, *and still join hands as Americans when it counts.* It was a powerful message.

But some on the left didn't see it that way. After eight long years with President George W. Bush, liberal activists and some of the president's own staff did not want someone like Warren to have a seat at the table in this White House too. So a campaign began to defame Warren and pressure the president to disinvite one of America's most popular and well-known pastors. People for the American Way said the president's invite to Warren was "a genuine blow to LGBT Americans."[1] The editor of the *Washington Blade* called it Obama's "first big mistake."[2] Joe Solmonese, president of Human Rights Campaign, explained the response: "There is a lot of energy and there's a lot of anger and I think people are wanting to direct it somewhere."[3]

President Obama did not cave; the campaign handled the crisis as one would expect. On December 18, 2008, the president gave a press conference in which he responded to a question about his choice of Rick Warren by affirming that his campaign's message was that while "we're not going to agree on every single issue, [we need] to create an atmosphere where we can disagree without being disagreeable and then focus on those things that we hold in common as Americans."[4]

This was the president who would bring Americans together. This was Obama at his best. He affirmed diversity and the big tent of the American family, he affirmed his support of LGBT inclusion by asking Bishop Gene Robinson—the first openly gay bishop in the Episcopal Church—to pray during official inauguration events, and he showed Americans how we can all live together despite our deep differences. Pastor Warren delivered a prayer that was respectful and unifying, and millions of American evangelicals felt included in the inauguration of a progressive, pro-LGBT president. ABC News reported Warren's prayer set an "inclusive tone" and reported on how the moment suggested a potential end to the culture wars.[5]

One reporter shared the general feeling of disappointment felt by those who thought Rick Warren might browbeat the crowd:

> As many have said, Warren just prayed, he wasn't trying to convert anybody or espouse any perceived "anti-gay" message. In fact, as he prayed, you saw people with hands outstretched, crying. They were taken with the moment. It was a testament to Obama's inclusion of people of all views.[6]

WHAT A DIFFERENCE A TERM MAKES

Four years later, Louie Giglio—and the many Americans who identify with him—did not get the same treatment.

Louie Giglio is the pastor of Passion City Church, founder of sixstepsrecords (a popular Christian record label), an author, and an evangelist through the Passion movement. His ministry touches the lives of millions of people around the world.

Despite what the reports suggested, he was not an unknown commodity in the White House. In a meeting with one of the president's senior advisors in 2012, I shared the press clip from the Passion conference that had taken place earlier that week. As CNN and other outlets reported, sixty thousand college students packed out the Georgia Dome and raised $3 million to combat human trafficking. It was an incredible display of commitment from young evangelicals who view modern-day slavery as one of the great injustices of their lifetime.

We discussed the president's statement to Rick Warren at

the 2008 Civil Forum on the Presidency that as president he would work to combat human trafficking. The administration had already taken action on the issue, but there had not been a real effort to use the bully pulpit to raise the profile on the issue. Senior staff agreed.

Within a few weeks the president cited Passion City Church in his National Prayer Breakfast speech. Louie was meeting with staffers in the National Security Council. He delivered a prayer at the president's Easter Prayer Breakfast in April 2012, just a few feet from where the president was sitting in a room full of senior White House officials and our nation's top religious leaders. He sat at the president's table. The White House pursued Louie, and Louie graciously served where he could.

There was significant progress on fighting modern-day slavery as well. You can draw a straight line from the administration's learning about Louie's leadership on the issue to the president delivering the longest speech on slavery of any American president since Abraham Lincoln at the Clinton Global Initiative just two months before Election Day. For the first time, the President's Interagency Task Force to Monitor and Combat Trafficking in Persons met at the White House rather than some conference room at the State Department.

A 2016 report on the administration's effort to combat trafficking pointed to his 2012 speech as the impetus for their efforts and listed millions in new financial commitments, policy advancements, and public/private partnerships to combat trafficking in the areas of rule of law, public awareness, victim services, and addressing procurement and supply chains that resulted from the new focus.

Louie was a part of all of this, yet when he was suggested

as the inaugural speaker, I was uneasy. Louie was and continues to be a friend, and I knew his mission was about provoking the hearts of young people. He was not a politician and did not seem to me to be the kind of person to filter his actions through a political lens. But, after I was pressed, I conceded: "I guess if the vet comes back clean, there's nothing to worry about."

I could not have been more wrong.

The White House vet came back clean—meaning that the professional researchers looked into Louie's history and found nothing disqualifying or particularly problematic—and Louie accepted the president's invitation.

Once I heard the White House was moving forward with the request, I started to feel like it was a fitting end to my time with the president. I had entered politics because of civil rights, and the invocation was going to be delivered by Myrlie Evers-Williams, the widow of Medgar Evers, a hero and martyr of the civil rights movement. The whole message of pairing Myrlie Evers-Williams with Louie Giglio was to draw a line from one movement for human dignity, the civil rights movement, with another, the fight against modern slavery.

The selection of Louie also seemed fitting because Louie was precisely the type of evangelical leader that had been core to my outreach at the White House. When I came to the White House, I realized that the prevailing incentive for religious engagement was to lift up leaders and organizations that were willing to use their infrastructure to support the administration electorally. This was and often continues to be part of the vicious cycle of a partisan faith and a politics where religion is used as a wedge. Religious leaders gain access by politicizing their ministries, politicians give these leaders influence, the media suggests these partisan religious figures are the most important religious leaders, and the cycle goes on. The faith leaders doing good work, leading well, and cultivating their faith communities usually do not pursue political influence, and so their perspective is not included as policymakers make decisions. To the extent that we believe Christians know something about flourishing and the human condition, this kind of Christian political disengagement means the communities in which we live lose out on something of great value.

In the White House, I centered our evangelical outreach on those serving and doing the work that reflected the evangelicalism familiar to those outside of press conferences and political rallies. Religion had become polarized in our country, in part, because we were only hearing from polarizing religious leaders. Instead of an outreach focused on mollifying politically mobilized conservatives or getting involved in evangelical theological fights in order to lift the profiles of the most liberal evangelical leaders, our outreach focused on those whom faithful evangelicals recognized as their leaders and on those who were contributing to the national good.

Louie represented twenty-first-century evangelical leadership. He held views that aren't fashionable, as all religious people usually will, but he used his platform to bring people together, and he kept the focus on Jesus, not politics. He was willing to work with anyone on common goals. He was willing to pray with a president many other evangelicals cursed. He was, in many ways, the type of evangelical leader Democrats had pined for just years ago when they were on the defensive with the faith community. They just wanted someone who would stop hitting them over the head with social issues.

But now liberals were the sharks who smelled blood in the water.

My bosses at the inaugural committee found out about the selection from the White House and complained that they were not consulted. Almost immediately after the selection of Louie was announced, a liberal blog[7] had audio and the transcript of remarks Louie had made in 1994 at a youth conference, in which he described homosexuality as sin.[8] I wondered if the blogger's fast response was possible because he was given a heads-up about Louie from "loyal" staff on the inaugural committee.

What followed was easily the worst period of my time working for the president. I sat in conference rooms listening to communications and outreach colleagues lecture me on what kind of man Louie was based on a sound bite from twenty years earlier. After the successes in the 2012 election legalizing same-sex marriage in several states, some liberal groups wanted to assert their power. They offered an ultimatum: We stayed quiet on Chuck Hagel, your nomination for defense secretary, even though he supported "don't ask, don't tell." Keep Giglio, and we won't stay quiet on Hagel any longer.

It became clear that some of the senior staff on the inaugural committee felt this was their opportunity to correct what they viewed as the president's errant choice of Rick Warren four years previously. Preventing Louie from delivering the benediction was progress to them, a signal of how far we had come.

Indeed, the other message liberal groups wanted to send was that after years of Republicans using LGBT issues as a bludgeon to shame and beat Democrats into submission, it was now their turn—it was time for conservatives to feel like outcasts.

In the final hours before Louie ultimately withdrew from consideration, I was scrambling. Running on no sleep and a lot of coffee, I received a call from one of the few people I knew who had earned the trust of both LGBT groups and evangelicals. The conflict over Louie ran directly against his bridge-building work, and he had wanted to see if he could help calm the waters. He told me that he had just gotten off the phone with senior staff at one of our country's leading LGBT rights groups. After deciding a truce on Louie was impossible, he'd asked the senior staffer what kind of religious leader would be acceptable to replace Louie. The activist replied, "Honestly, if it is a Christian, we will find something on him, and we will make him famous."

This sounds like something from the television series *House of Cards*. But it was real life. I left the office and thought about never coming back. I almost did not.

I made a few calls to friends and colleagues I trusted and decided that with just days left until the inauguration, and more than six years of working for the president, I should stay and finish well.

I still wonder if I made the right choice.

For the Left, the options were clear: either Louie would be pressured to recant his remarks in full, or he would be forced to withdraw. Some friends were urging Louie to refuse to withdraw and force the White House to publicly disinvite him. They wanted a showdown.

I still felt at this time that if the president got personally involved, he would uphold his principle of inclusion and unity as he had in his first inauguration. There was a part of me that wanted a showdown too.

But I also knew that the fallout of such a stand by Louie would be unpredictable. Sure, maybe the president would decline to disinvite him in light of his stated convictions and past actions in similar situations, but I had no doubt that an "anonymous administration source" would be quoted in the *Times* or the *Post* stating on the president's behalf that Louie was no longer wanted. The torrent of accusations cast on Louie in the weeks leading up to the inauguration would have been overwhelming, and if he made it to the inaugural stage, there would be planned protests that moved the focus from God and prayer to politics and division.

Louie also wasn't interested in making a political point. He had accepted the president's invitation out of a sense of graciousness and partnership, not to use it as a platform for political involvement. His calling to reach young people with the gospel was clear and explicit.

On the longest night, the night before Louie withdrew, I heard from my desk senior political staff on the Inaugural Committee loudly mock an e-mail from one of the president's faith advisors explaining that Louie was "not a culture warrior." But these illustrious staffers had read a blog post or two on Louie. They knew for themselves what was true.

What they did not know, what very few people knew, is that Louie's engagement with the president and the White House was not just around efforts to prevent human trafficking. Just days after President Obama announced his support for same-sex marriage, Obama held a private meeting with four evangelical leaders to discuss how to move forward in a way that promoted unity, not division. That meeting included Gabe Lyons, Tim Keller, and Louie Giglio.[9] Louie was personally invited by the

White House to talk with the president about his views on the very set of issues that would justify his exclusion from the inaugural ceremony months later.

In a statement, Louie announced he was withdrawing from the inaugural ceremony, doing so in hopes of ending the political story as quickly as possible and in a way that attempted to remove all responsibility from the president and his staff. It was a generous statement.

Unfortunately, the statement from the Inaugural Committee, drafted without my involvement, did not share his spirit of generosity. No clearer example of the difference between how much things had changed over four years, how much the president had changed, can be found than a comparison of the statements regarding Warren and Giglio.

In 2009, the president said that part of the message of his whole campaign was "that we're not going to agree on every single issue, but what we have to do is to be able to create an atmosphere when we—where we can disagree without being disagreeable and then focus on those things that we hold in common as Americans." He continued: "And that's, hopefully, going to be a spirit that carries over into my administration."[10]

It clearly did not in this case. Now the language of diversity and inclusion was used to justify exclusion:

> We were not aware of Pastor Giglio's past comments at the time of his selection and they don't reflect our desire to celebrate the strength and diversity of our country at this Inaugural. Pastor Giglio was asked to deliver the benediction in large part for his leadership in combating human trafficking around the world. As we now work to select

someone to deliver the benediction, we will ensure their beliefs reflect this administration's vision of inclusion and acceptance for all Americans.[11]

In 2009, our diversity demanded we accept that there will be voices we disagree with in public spaces. In 2013, diversity required us to expel dissent.

Not only was this an astounding reversal from 2009, it was also a rejection of the position we'd taken at the Democratic convention just months earlier. Unlike a national ceremony, a party convention actually has no requirement for ideological diversity. Yet there was Cardinal Timothy Dolan, head of the United States Conference of Catholic Bishops, praying from the podium as part of a political message of inclusion. Cardinal Dolan represented a church that had some pretty clear things to say about issues such as abortion and homosexuality, but he was included to solve a political problem.

In 2009, we had true pluralism and the big American tent. In 2012, at the Democratic convention, we had a pretense of inclusion and magnanimity for political gain. In 2013, with our last four years in hand and the "weight of history on our side" that pretense went out the window. Now the Democratic Party was about consolidation.

I supported, in the president's interest, selecting Reverend Luis León as the replacement. Reverend León is the rector at St. John's Episcopal Church, which sits directly across from the White House across Lafayette Park. The president had attended the church several times during his presidency, often walking with the First Lady, Malia, and Sasha across the beautiful park in their Sunday best. Reverend León was as close as possible to a choice without a message.

The inauguration prayers went off without a hitch, and the president delivered one of his most assertive, progressive speeches of his presidency. There was no real backlash for how the administration handled the benediction controversy, at least not one they would feel. To them, it seemed as if the same old people were complaining once again, while most of their allies were happy.

My last day working for the president was the National Prayer Service the day after the inauguration. I had spent the night before at the inaugural balls and maybe slept for an hour before waking up at three thirty in the morning for one final trip in the eerie stillness of morning twilight. After the service, I saw the president on his way out. He said he enjoyed Reverend Adam Hamilton's sermon that morning and wanted a copy. We shook hands and I told him what an honor it was to serve him.

It was over.

CHAPTER 11

REAL HOPE

I hung around the cathedral to say hello to visiting clergy, but there were only so many people to talk to until there was no more talking to do.

I walked across the street to one of my favorite restaurants, 2Amys. When I had first arrived in Washington, I was told that it was the only restaurant in the area that was officially recognized by the Italian government to sell Neapolitan-style pizza.

The restaurant was almost empty—it was barely noon. For the first moment in six years, I had no pressing demands on my time. I was forced to look back.

In a matter of minutes, I'd gone from shaking hands with the president to sitting at a restaurant bar in the middle of the work-day. Unemployed. Sleep deprived. Wearied.

After all the highs and disappointments, the stress and the elation, I was now at a point of separation from all that I experienced. It was here that I could begin to discover with clear eyes the answer to the question that has haunted and enlivened so many throughout human history: what can I hope for?

WHAT IS HOPE?

The word *hope* is ubiquitous in our age. It is slogan. It is propaganda. It is comfort. It was a message of hope that propelled Barack Obama to the national stage and later to the presidency.

What does it mean to hope?

Hope takes many forms, ranging from small and personal ("I hope I get a parking space") to the large and social ("We hope to eradicate modern slavery through this legislation"), but there is a particular kind of hope that transcends them all. This is a hope that psychologist Herbert Plugge identified in his work with patients who attempted suicide or were incurably ill, a "fundamental" or "authentic" hope that, as one historian of Plugge's work said, "is not directed toward anything that one could 'have' but rather has something to do with what one 'is.'"[1] Moreover, Plugge suggests authentic hope only arrives once our other hopes—whether personal or social—are found insufficient or false. I think this is where I found myself that morning in the restaurant. When our little hopes are disappointed, we find ourselves situated between the harshness of despair and the daunting, unusual existence of real hope.

TA-NEHISI COATES AND HOPE

Ta-Nehisi Coates's *Between the World and Me* was published in 2015 to resounding acclaim. The book—presented as a letter to his son about navigating the world as a black boy and man—won the 2015 National Book Award for Nonfiction. The book is a powerful, deeply moving work, and Coates is a writer whose thinking demands attention regardless of the topic.

However, if there was any critique of the book that was shared by both conservatives and liberals, it was Coates's lack of hope. In fact, he rejects hope outright. Addressing his son, he wrote:

> You must resist the common urge toward the comforting narrative of divine law, toward fairy tales that imply some irrepressible justice. The enslaved were not bricks in your road, and their lives were not chapters in your redemptive history. They were people turned to fuel for the American machine. Enslavement was not destined to end, and it is wrong to claim our present circumstance—no matter how improved—as the redemption for the lives of people who never asked for the posthumous, untouchable glory of dying for their children. Our triumphs can never redeem this. Perhaps our triumphs are not even the point. Perhaps struggle is all we have. So you must wake up every morning knowing that no natural promise is unbreakable, least of all the promise of waking up at all. This is not despair. These are the preferences of the universe itself: verbs over nouns, actions over states, struggle over hope.[2]

Conservative writers critiqued Coates's rejection of hope in ways that were both dismissive[3] and earnest.[4] Progressives critiqued Coates, too, primarily on the grounds that his vision of struggle offers no expectation that there is "any hope of breaking once and for all the history and cycle of racial oppression in

America."[5] Coates wrote in response to this kind of critique, "a writer wedded to 'hope' is ultimately divorced from 'truth.'"[6]

When confronted with the reality of pain and injustice, a hope that is not grounded in reality as well is insufficient. Is there an answer to Coates's challenge? What is the place of hope in history?

HOPE IN HUMAN PROGRESS

There are two dominant conceptions of hope in modern Western thought: the hope of human progress and religious hope, and specifically to our interest here, Christian hope.

Hope rooted in human progress is an old idea, rooted in the Enlightenment of the eighteenth and nineteenth centuries. It was a hope that both grew out of and seemed confirmed by the scientific and technological progress of the era. But as many observers have noted, hope in human progress was challenged and swamped by the events of the twentieth century: the World Wars, the Holocaust, and Jim Crow. At precisely the time when those who hailed the inexorable march of human progress expected perfection to appear on the horizon, the Western world expanded our firsthand knowledge of man's capacity for evil, oppression, and death. Perhaps no twentieth-century development looms larger than that of nuclear weapons, which hold the possibility of humanity destroying itself. The advance of technology, which has certainly brought us many great things—penicillin and other medical developments, flight, modern communications, and so on—has also ushered in new forms of evil.

These historical realities actually gave way to an embrace of hopelessness among intellectuals that remains at the surface of our public discourse even when shrouded with a thin veil of "hope talk." And who can blame them? In light of horrors of the last century, can we really hope at all?

CHRISTIAN HOPE

Christian hope has, for many, become meaningless, confused with false and little hopes that do little more than put a spiritual gauze on the material and temporal. But what is actual Christian hope?

Christian hope is both individual and corporate, personal and universal. It is a hope that reaches across time, from the past to eternity without skipping over this very present moment in our lives.

In individual terms, it is a hope for personal redemption and salvation. Christians believe in the reality of sin, and in a God who can be sinned against. To sin is to act against the will of God or to refuse to act in accordance with it. Sin creates a chasm between us and God, so Jesus came as a complete, perfect atonement to reconcile the gap between us and the presence and will of God. Christians thus have assurance that our future is secured, that we will join with Jesus in His resurrection, and that we will rest and act and worship and love in the full presence of God and each other forever. This is what Paul meant when he wrote that not even death can separate us from the love of Christ (Romans 8:38). Jesus alone provides sufficient grounds to hope in the face of hope's ultimate challenge: death.

The life Jesus offers gives us reason to hope in the here and now, hope both for ourselves individually and for all of creation. This hope is rooted in Jesus' announcement at the start of His ministry that He is ushering in a kingdom used by God for His purposes of justice and mercy. He announced an era of possibility that affects people of all faiths and none. We can count on the fact that God is at work on behalf of justice and mercy, and we are invited to work with Him, drawing on the strength He provides (1 Peter 4:11) with the knowledge our work will not go to waste (1 Corinthians 15:58). God promises to be with us in the present, and so our present is as secure as our future. The point of our lives, therefore, is not to make peace with the inevitability of death but to reconcile with life.

HOPE, HISTORY, AND THE MORAL ARC OF THE UNIVERSE

The quote is now familiar to most of us: "The arc of the moral universe is long, but it bends towards justice." The sentence is woven into the carpet in the Oval Office—I looked at it whenever I was in the room. It is a part of our political dialogue now, used to bless a whole range of political solutions.

The sentence is often attributed to Reverend Martin Luther King Jr., but King was quoting another clergyman, Theodore Parker. Parker wrote in the early nineteenth century that from what he could see that arc "bends towards justice" and reminds readers that "things refuse to be mismanaged long. Jefferson trembled when he thought of slavery and remembered that God is just. Ere long all America will tremble."[7] King used a version of the phrase in an article for a Christian newsletter over a century later, but what remained constant was its connection to the initiative and involvement of God. In context, he wrote, "Those of us who call the name of Jesus Christ find something at the center of our faith which forever reminds us that God is on the side of truth and justice. . . . Good Friday may occupy the throne for a day, but ultimately it must give way to the triumphant beat of the drums of Easter. Evil may so shape events that Caesar will occupy a palace and Christ a cross, but that same Christ will rise up and split history into A.D. and B.C., so that even the life of Caesar must be dated by his name. Yes, 'the arc of the moral universe is long, but it bends toward justice.'"[8]

This idea was only intelligible to King when joined with a confidence in Christ, and in God's nature and faithfulness. The arc of the moral universe does not bend toward justice because of a political program or the unassailable motives of humans, but because of a God who wills justice. History, then, is not about human progress but, as one theologian put it, about God "breaking into human history to establish his reign and to advance his purposes."[9]

This is why Christians so often talk about following God's will, for they acknowledge God's ever-present invitation to be a part of His ongoing work in renewing and making whole this world, the very environment we experience today. It is hope that makes way for us, not the other way around. There is indeed an arc to the moral universe, but it is not a matter of humanity progressing toward justice; rather, it is the God of justice who is moving toward us. This hope opens our eyes to the present.

COATES AND HOPE

Ta-Nehisi Coates was confronted with precisely this vision of hope, first in print and then in person. Pastor Thabiti Anyabwile, pastor of Anacostia River Church in Washington, DC, wrote a response to Coates's book in the *Atlantic*, the same publication where Coates is employed. Anyabwile expressed unqualified support for Coates's analysis of various injustices but suggested Coates had failed his readers by not offering hope. Anyabwile recalled the "arc of the moral universe" and noted Coates's utter, explicit rejection of the idea in *Between the World and Me* in writing, "My understanding of the universe was physical, and its moral arc bent toward chaos then concluded in a box."[10]

Anyabwile responded with the evidence of hope in the African American story: "Hope was beneath the respectable Sunday-best attire worn to civil-rights marches. Hope was undergirding calls for respectable self-control among sit-in demonstrators while being inhumanely sprayed with condiments at lunch counters. Hope was resting in the weary hearts of respectable marchers and demonstrators packed in jail cells following protests." He concluded: "Hope is not an abstraction or an escapist fantasy. Sometimes hope is the only real asset the oppressed have."[11]

Coates subsequently interviewed Anyabwile at a conference on racial issues hosted by the *Atlantic*. Coates, as gracious and committed to intellectual pursuit as ever, asked Anyabwile to make his case for hope. At a secular event and as the only explicitly religious speaker at the entire conference, Anyabwile said the following: "My sort of case for hope builds on the fact that there is coming the greatest, most perfect criminal justice ever known. That when Christ comes and establishes his reign, there will be no more injustice, there will be no more crime. Everything that has been crooked will be made straight."[12]

Coates asked Anyabwile what his case for hope was for those who don't share his faith. Anyabwile responded first by saying that "hope is one of those things that is, I think, given to us as a gift by virtue of being human. Many people hope in many different things and people have varying reasons for hope, so at the most basic level, I want to encourage that." But he then returned to his earlier point, that "our faith is only as good as the object of our faith. All the other things that we put our hope and trust in, short of God himself, are going to be, in the final analysis, inadequate for our biggest hopes."[13]

Note that Anyabwile's hope is not utilitarian, not simply a source of motivation, but rather a reflection of reality: that Jesus came, He is at work today, and He will return. Coates followed him right to that point and said, "I think what I'm left with here is that those of us who don't necessarily share the same religious belief are left without a firm hope. Isn't that the upshot of what you're offering?" Again, Anyabwile responded to earnestness with earnestness, not dancing around the point, and told Coates, "I think there is a sense in which that is true. That is just a sort of unpleasant consequence of my line of reasoning."[14]

At this point, a member of the audience laughed loudly, so the pastor continued, to prevent laughter from allowing an evasion of the question. "We laugh and we sort of feel a way about that, but we all have to follow our logic to its conclusion," Anyabwile said as Coates looked on inquisitively with his hand supporting his head.[15] To the person who does not have religious faith, Anyabwile explained, he would say, "Talk to me about the types of things you do hope in, and let's talk about how far that gets you to your best hopes, your best dreams." He observed that he often finds in conversations with nonbelievers that when they "start to peep over the precipice and see the despair at the end of unbelief then they back up . . . and very often they want to trade in the currency of faith, and in the currency of belief, without actually ascribing to it. So here is where the conversation gets hard for everyone. . . . We have to push each other to our natural conclusions."[16]

As the course of the conversation that followed revealed—and as his writings make clear—Coates is not like those who "trade in the currency of faith . . . without ascribing to it." Unlike those individuals, Coates does not argue for hope in something other than God; rather, he "argues for chaos," since for Coates there is in the universe no directing force that justifies hope in anything.

With the final word in the brief conversation, Anyabwile asked the audience to look at the world around them. "Our lives are not as chaotic as all that. All of us experience boundaries to the chaos, and order in the chaos. We don't live in a disorganized universe, ultimately, and that is because there's an Organizer. And that's because there's One who governs history and governs the world . . . and my suggestion would be: put your hope in that One."[17]

HOPE IN A SECULAR AGE

The conversation was not an easy one, and it did not end with Coates's conversion to Anyabwile's faith. But it is a conversation that Christians have had for a long time. Real hope is a challenge to the way we live our lives and to the idols we hold. As was noted by theologian Jurgen Moltmann, "It is not for nothing that at the entrance to Dante's hell there stand the words 'Abandon hope, all ye who enter here.'"[18]

The possibilities hope opens up are available to everyone. The question is not whether people who do not believe in Jesus have reason to hope. The question at hand is that if Jesus is the only one who can truly bear a person's hopes, why would a person not embrace that hope? Coates's line of questioning rested on the assumption that Christianity was for Christians, and that Anyabwile's argument had no relevance to those not "in the tribe." But Christianity is an abolishment of tribes. It is radical in its openness and, therefore, in its application.

If there cannot be alignment on what our hope is *in*, there can certainly be more alignment in what Christians and non-Christians hope *for*, though our different starting places will often affect our means. We can hope that someone might be healed, or a relationship might be strengthened. We can hope for social goods together too. I have taken part in, and helped to facilitate, many interfaith coalitions that express a common hope for something even if the reason for hope among its participants was different. Christians ought to seek partnerships with people of all faiths (and none) who are willing to work together for peace, justice, and compassion. Christian hopes can be advanced by non-Christian sources, even government, and Christians can be confident in embracing what is good, because we know God is at work in all things.

Christians must be careful, though, to never confuse their plans for God's plans. As Christians see it, the hope of humanity is Christ, not humanity. And that hope is challenged in our day. Dr. Raphael Warnock—who preaches from the pulpit at Ebenezer Baptist Church where Dr. King was pastor—has said, "It takes a tough mind and a tender heart to hold on to hope."[19] But hold on we must. Hope is our tether to reality, and our bulwark against despair.

Christian hope is both with and beyond history. We know there is hope for history, because God has been and is acting in it. Hope not only reaches across time, but it reaches from outside of time itself. History will not culminate with the end of a long march of human progress toward perfection but with God redeeming all things.

It is precisely at the time when the truth of hope is challenged that Christians are called to speak of hope with a joyful confidence. Christians need not be defensive: it is Christ who is our defense (Psalm 59:9). We need not pine for the past like those who have no hope: our future is caught up in Christ (1 Thessalonians 4:13, 17). Our call is to be faithful today, in light of the hope that has been given to us.

HOPE AND POSSIBILITY

It was tempting that morning alone in the restaurant to contemplate my future, to look back at all I had experienced and come away with the conclusion that I was at the end of the book, rather than the beginning of a new chapter. I certainly did not have everything figured out when I left the restaurant that afternoon, but I did know this: God was not finished. He is still at work, and that means I still have work to do too.

Hope is always reclaiming; it is always transforming that which was a wasteland, which was previously thought unfit for use, into something that can be cultivated, which can yield a harvest. When the pundits and prognosticators say we should withdraw, that there is no way forward, hope gives us the eyes to see new possibility. It is this new vision, a gift from hope, that will allow us to see our politics anew.

CHAPTER 12

RECLAIMING HOPE

As someone who has experienced firsthand the great successes and bitter disappointments that politics brings, I can say without equivocation that politics is not where you want to place your hope. People who place their hope in politics are idealists who then become cynics, and there is rarely a resting stop on that journey. We need to have a firmer ground to stand upon when engaging in politics than politics itself.

I am proud of the work I did at the White House. I served the president and his faith-based office well, with as much dedication as I knew how to give. I certainly made mistakes. I should have spent more time building relationships with other departments that would have strengthened my work. There were meetings I'm sure I could have been better prepared for, and tactics that might have been more effective. There are e-mails I wish I could have back and calls I wish I had made.

I also have had time to think more philosophically and theologically about my work. What does it mean to write or contribute to a speech for someone else on what he or she believes? About policy? About God?

Here is a tough question: To what extent did my service in the Obama administration give people a false impression of the president's goals and convictions? This is actually a common question. A central theme of former Obama administration transportation secretary and Republican Ray LaHood's memoir is his attempt to reconcile his confidence in the sincerity of the president's desire to quell partisanship with the concrete actions taken that stoked it.[1]

Ambassador Samantha Power, who is a hero to many for her work to combat and prevent genocide, is another example of this tension. In a profile of Power, a former senior White House aide was quoted anonymously: "Are people like her around to give credibility, though they're actually not listened to? I think that's a fair question, and I don't know what the answer is."[2] David Rothkopf, the editor of *Foreign Policy*, said that while Power "could be the North Star to some extent, she actually ends up being a kind of counterpoint, illustrating the fact that they are not, for the most part, living up to their convictions."[3]

These two examples are, of course, only relevant to my case in a limited sense. LaHood and Power were cabinet officials, and Power in particular, has had a long-standing personal relationship of respect with Obama. They were both in positions of senior-level leadership with far more levers of power at their disposal. To be straightforward and obvious about it, they were both more important in government than I was. I did not have a national public reputation as a champion for bipartisanship or for human rights interventions. I raise their examples to help flesh out the complexities of working at the White House as a political appointee at any level.

In the same profile of Ambassador Power, the reporter, Evan Osnos, asked her if she ever thought of stepping down. Power replied, "My basic view is that there is an awful lot of good that one can do in these jobs, and you have to look at the composite. . . . I'm conscious of the risk of self-rationalization and self-perpetuation and so forth. But this is not a close call to me."

I generally agree with Power's assessment when I think about my role. When I was at the White House, my role was to serve the president, and that was evident to those inside and outside the White House. It's in the job description. And I did my best to fulfill my responsibilities with integrity. I served the president with loyalty, and I was honest and forthright in my outreach with religious leaders. When I served in the White House, I never unilaterally leaked news when things did not go my way, and I never acted outside of my role in the faith-based office. My work led to concrete benefits for the American people. And most of all, I sought to be faithful to God. Since I have left the White House, I have tried to steward my influence well in light of both my previous service in government, and the fact that my ultimate allegiance is not to any political party.

While I am convinced that we should not place our hope in politics, what I also know from seeing our politics up close is that our nation benefits greatly from people carrying hope—real hope, one rooted in reality—with them into the public square.

So, we must ask, what are the consequences, the obligations, of hope in our public lives? What does a hopeful politics look like?

WHY POLITICS?

The very nature of the American system of government assumes the individual call to citizenship. This duty is not a favor from the government but a responsibility. It is part of the social contract each citizen shares with his or her government and fellow citizens. Regardless of a person's religious affiliation, as citizens we are appointed co-caretakers of our system of government. Therefore, consideration of how we engage in politics and public life (which is discussed later in this chapter) is relevant to all people.

Christian political obligations derive from love of God and love of neighbor. Scripture is filled with reminders of our obligation to look out for the welfare of others, but Jeremiah's exhortation to the exiles in Babylon in Jeremiah 29 is especially instructive. These people, God's people, found themselves in a land that was not their own among a people who despised them. Yet, Jeremiah's prophecy to them did not suggest that they "lie low" or that they take a posture of opposition toward the Babylonians. Instead, they are instructed to "seek the peace and prosperity of the city to which I have carried you into exile. Pray to the LORD for it, because if it prospers, you too will prosper."⁴ For Christians, one inescapable conclusion of this extraordinary command is that we are obliged to work for the benefit and the flourishing of all people, whether or not they see the world as we do or agree with us in any way. Christians' obligation is not to their "tribe," but to their God—a God who cares deeply for all people. If a Christian's political ideas and actions are not intended toward the good of their "enemies," their political witness is not Christian in its character. When it is, the entire body politic benefits.

When Jesus came centuries later, He ushered in a new era of

good news for all people, not just as individuals, but for the world. Near the beginning of His ministry, Jesus shocked and angered those in a Nazarene synagogue by reading from the prophet Isaiah: "The Spirit of the Lord is on me, because he has anointed me to proclaim good news to the poor. He has sent me to proclaim freedom for the prisoners and recovery of sight for the blind, to set the oppressed free, to proclaim the year of the Lord's favor."[5] The meaning of this is as clear as it is revolutionary: Jesus came to redeem not just souls, but all things. And the new life that He has welcomed us into is not to be lived in isolation from others.

Jesus' commission to the public square can be found in Matthew 5, where He says to His disciples: "You are the salt of the earth. . . . You are the light of the world. A town built on a hill cannot be hidden. Neither do people light a lamp and put it under a bowl. Instead they put it on its stand, and it gives light to everyone in the house. In the same way, let your light shine before others, that they may see your good deeds and glorify your Father in heaven."[6]

If Christians are to truly address the circumstances of the voiceless, the oppressed, and the vulnerable, we must acknowledge that while prayer and private acts of kindness and compassion are essential, an approach that includes only these tools is incomplete. So many of the problems in our communities, our nation, and our world are a result not only of individual negligence but of corporate malpractice and systemic depravity. An earnest attempt to follow the scriptural commands mentioned above will include public and political approaches. A holistic pursuit of justice and the well-being of our neighbors is inconceivable without political involvement. Politics is one of the essential forums in which we can love our neighbor.

So Christians are led to politics by this logic: we know that we are to seek the good of our city and nation, and we are therefore motivated to seek the good in our politics as well.

HOPE IN PUBLIC

Hope Looks Like Commitment

In America, individualism has always been in creative tension with the power and authority of institutions. At its best, this tension makes both better: our institutions benefit from individuals' discontent with the status quo, and Americans benefit from the depth of thought and supportive structures that only institutions can provide. We are now out of balance. Our institutions are starved by a perspective that views withdrawal and a rejection of institutional commitments as an act of righteousness.

In American politics, we see this most clearly in the rise of political independents. The percentage of Americans who are political independents is at an all-time high: 43 percent.[7] Fifty percent of millennials are independents.[8] We have a number of slogans used to describe independent voters: they think for themselves, they're prophets daring to shout "a pox on both your houses," they are rejecting the false set of choices Washington gives us and transforming our politics. Like many popular slogans, however, these statements are simply not true.

In a two-party system of government, in a party-based system of government of any kind, to become an independent is to check out of the system. It is to unilaterally disarm, to give up one of the primary levers we have as citizens to influence our political system. Withdrawal is not a prophetic message that those in power ought to shape up. They are not listening. Your voice is not heard when you don't show up.

Some wonder why our political parties have become more extreme, why Congress is in a stalemate and compromise is nowhere to be found. A major reason is that many of the people who would provide either of our political parties with some semblance of balance have left the party altogether. This is not an abstract or symbolic argument. In many states, you cannot vote in a party's presidential primary unless you belong to that party. You cannot become a party delegate and vote on the party platform unless you belong to that party.

Our political institutions are built for our participation, but they do not require it. This is their weakness and their worth. Christians, who are called to love their neighbor and to seek their good, must consider what it looks like to those neighbors when we check out of the political system. For all Americans, who inherit the rights and duties of citizenship from previous generations who have paid a price, what does withdrawal look like to your neighbor?

John Stott, the brilliant British theologian and a father of the modern evangelical movement, wrote that "when society does go bad, we Christians tend to throw up our hands in pious horror and reproach the non-Christian world; but should we not rather reproach ourselves? One can hardly blame unsalted meat for going bad. It cannot do anything else. The real question to ask is: where is the salt?"[9]

Withdrawal from politics and our political parties is not the answer. The Republican Party needs now more than ever Christians advocating from within for a position, for example, on immigration reform that respects human dignity and takes the consequences of deportation on families seriously. The

Democratic Party needs now more than ever Christians advocating from within for a recognition, say, that abortion is not a moral good, that it is not how a just society addresses unintended pregnancies, and that a respect for human dignity and a sense of protecting the vulnerable extends to those not yet born. The Christian's duty in politics is the same as every citizen's: to affirm what is good and speak out against that which is not.

Christians must not cordon off God from any area of our lives. Jesus is not bewildered by the political choices we face. He understands our political system perfectly. He is not daunted by the messiness and brokenness of our politics. We can navigate our political choices, depending on Him and the Holy Spirit, as we can in every area of our life. Therefore, we need not abdicate political commitments.

Hope Pursues Justice

When I was at the White House, I helped to convene a briefing for evangelical leaders with some of the most senior officials in the administration. Raj Shah, the head of the US Agency for International Development at the time, came by to speak to the group about a program called Feed the Future, a massive effort to combat global hunger. He is an unquestionably brilliant man who came to serve at USAID after a leading role at the Bill & Melinda Gates Foundation. He was known in government and by those who worked in international development as someone who was relatively unburdened by ideology—he just wanted to get things done and make an impact on the vast array of challenges facing the poor around the world.

Shah briefed the leaders on the Feed the Future program and opened it up to questions. After a few questions on the policy details, one individual in the meeting, a conservative, jumped into the conversation. Addressing the chief executive of a major Christian antipoverty organization, the conservative asked whether or not the CEO's organization would be able to do the same work as Feed the Future but at a lower cost. Self-interest would have had the executive talk about the great work his organization does and how much more they could do with additional resources. Self-interest would have had him boast about his organization's financial model and their efforts to reduce overhead cost. In a room of his peers, he could have puffed himself up and played into tropes about the failings of government in combating global poverty.

Instead, the executive looked up and said, "You know, I'm not sure if we could do it cheaper. What I do know is that we need all the help we can get to tackle this problem, and what the administrator has laid out sounds pretty good to me."

With that simple statement, the tension in the room was let out, and the rest of the meeting focused on what it might look like to have increased coordination between nongovernmental organizations (NGOs) among themselves, and between NGOs and the government in pursuit of shared goals.

The fact of the matter is that we have seen incredible progress on global poverty in just the last twenty years as a result of the investments of governments, the work of the private sector, and the generosity of individuals who donate to this work. From 1990 to 2010, the global poverty rate was cut in half.[10] On October 4, 2015, the World Bank forecast for the first time ever that the global poverty rate would fall below 10 percent.[11]

Hope not only spurs this work on but has the courage to identify justice in the present as a marker, a glimpse of the justice that is to come.

How can someone act for justice in our politics?

First, vote. Vote up and down the ballot. Vote not just in presidential elections but in off-year elections. Voting is the most imprecise expression of our personal politics, but it is one of the most fundamental. Your vote is the essential political expression of care for the future of your community and nation—and the well-being of your neighbor. You are not defined by your vote any more than you are defined by your political party so long as you place your allegiance elsewhere. Consider the experiences you have had and what you believe about politics; consider the passions God has placed on your heart; consider the needs of your community, and vote knowing that you do so with incomplete information about imperfect candidates that you analyze imperfectly. But do vote.

Second, individual action can have a real impact. Many Americans would be surprised how effective it can be to take the simple act of writing a letter to your elected officials on an issue of concern. Even at the federal level, members of Congress have staffers who have the responsibility of receiving, cataloging, and responding to constituent mail. If the office receives multiple letters on the same topic, the elected official will be notified so that he or she can be responsive to their constituents.

Third, you can personally get involved as a volunteer and as a local advocate. Attend your local Democratic or Republican party meeting. Write letters to the editor of your local newspaper. Organize your friends for a letter-writing campaign on an important issue. Host a small group at your church regarding Christian political engagement, and help fellow believers find their voices.

Finally, invest time, money, and talent in advocacy organizations and nonprofits that are active politically. You do not need to be a policy expert or to spend your days thinking about politics and advocacy to make a difference. You do not need to dedicate your life to politics to participate in politics, any more than a religious person needs to become a member of the clergy in order to truly be religious. By allowing these organizations to speak for you, you are strengthening your voice and the voices of others. These organizations, and the people who work for them, have expertise in influencing decision making. Remember the examples from earlier in this book: how the Circle of Protection protected important funding for international and domestic poverty programs; the voices of sixty thousand college students against modern-day slavery reaching the White House; the advocates who helped make the adoption tax credit permanent.

Time and time again, I witnessed individuals and organizations that benefit from the trust of entire constituencies make a real difference in political decision making. It is a heroic act to use one's own gifts and resources to exert influence through politics for the benefit of others, but it is also a responsibility of citizenship. This is what is meant when people call participatory government "ennobling": it makes the ordinary noble and the noble ordinary. In hope we understand that justice is God's work. He will see it come to pass and we have an invitation to join Him in that work. Through political commitments, we can use the influence we have to pursue justice.

Hope Looks like Humility

Hope should also inform the way we approach our political commitments and decisions, for our hope should lead us to humility. As I've argued, Christians have an obligation to be involved in politics, but we do not belong to our politics. Since our identity is not found in our politics, we are freed up to pursue unlikely alliances, consider other points of view, and love our political enemies. In hope and humility, we can partner with and learn from people of different faiths, backgrounds, and ideological perspectives and across racial boundaries. Hope opens these doors. Hopeful politics are inclusive, because hope is so open to possibility. We look for it everywhere.

A spirit of humility also allows us to act without the presumption that we have all the answers, as well as without the burden of needing all the answers before we act. We are careful not to confuse our preferred policies with essential Christian doctrine, lest we fall into the trap C. S. Lewis identified and pretend "God has spoken when He has not spoken."[12] This is not to say we are not responsible for our actions—good intentions are insufficient, and reckless political engagement is contradictory to the principles of citizenship and the demands of hope. Yet humility prevents us from a withdrawal premised on our fear of being wrong or our fear of political loss. Humility and conviction do not inherently oppose one another. There is a kind of courage that can only come from humility.

This humility—one that rejects arrogance and superiority and embraces responsibility and thoughtful conviction with courage—is desperately needed in our politics today.

TWO BIG ISSUES: RACE AND RELIGIOUS FREEDOM

In the coming years, two political and cultural issues will deeply affect how Christians act and are perceived in our nation. The first is the area of racial justice and reconciliation. Racial inequalities and injustices have become a greater part of our public discussion and politics in recent years, in large part due to the effective advocacy of young activists working around the country. Though our response to racism and discrimination facing various communities—Native Americans, Hispanic Americans, Arab Americans, immigrants and refugees, and others—is of crucial importance, too, the African American community is of particular relevance for reasons of national and church history.

Race

Racial inequalities reflect a history of intentional racial harm against African Americans in this country. African American unemployment is twice that of whites.[13] One out of three black men between the ages of eighteen and thirty is in jail, in prison, on probation, or on parole.[14] Black students are more likely to be held back in school than white students, more likely to drop out of high school, and less likely to be read to as often as their white peers.[15] Blacks are nearly twice as likely to have zero or negative net worth than whites.[16] Some politicians are still trying to disenfranchise African American voters fifty years after the Voting Rights Act of 1964 was signed into law.[17]

Character and personal responsibility certainly count, but they should not be counted on to make up for a program of land theft, for instance. A 2001 Associated Press investigation into the theft of black-owned land dating back to the antebellum period identified 406 victims, affecting more than 24,000 acres valued at tens of millions of dollars.[18]

Our nation is held back by racism and inequality in both lost opportunity and the cost to government from our criminal justice, foster care, and welfare systems, just to name a few. We have a moral responsibility to help all children reach their potential and, in particular, to remove any government-sanctioned hindrances that would hold them back.

This does not mean that there can be no disagreement about what policies are best to address these issues. Indeed, there is disagreement in the African American community, even among African American liberals, on what policies are best. "Broken windows policing," which is now commonly excoriated by many leaders—for legitimate reasons—was originally vehemently supported by many African American leaders as a way to help lift the burden crime-infested neighborhoods place on law-abiding African Americans. Black intellectuals who reject calls for men to be better fathers and young people to conduct themselves with dignity as "respectability politics" are contradicted in black church pulpits every Sunday. Race should not become, or continue to be, a weapon with which to bully people into specific policy positions.

What is not acceptable is silence or the repetition of tired slogans that ignore impediments to equality. We will rightly be judged as a nation by how we address these issues, and whether we can summon the courage and will to take action.

As for white evangelicals and the future of the American church, these issues take on a special character. We cannot read Martin Luther King Jr.'s "Letter from a Birmingham Jail" without feeling pangs of shame and guilt, and if we linger on the thought too long, we'll feel much more than that.

I have been a part of many Christian conversations on racial reconciliation, and they often focus on the need to have more diverse relationships and churches. A multicultural church movement exists today that is beautiful and necessary. We need diverse churches in a nation where people are in multicultural families and live in constant contact with other ethnic and racial groups and experiences. I support the multicultural church movement, and I want to see it grow.

That said, I also know the power of the black church as it is and as it has been. The historically black denominations were created to provide a space and voice for people from a specific perspective and culture. It is a tradition that has played a specific role in fighting for justice and providing dignity to folks who had often been denied it by their fellow man. It was the unique, uncompromising, and prophetic witness of the black church that God used to draw me to Him more than a decade ago. As one pastor of an African Methodist Episcopal (AME) church said at a gathering on racial reconciliation I attended, "I love the AME Church. I am not leaving my church. God is moving in my church." We need diverse churches with diverse identities and expressions. If we have in our minds a goal for every church to be a kaleidoscope of races, not only are we setting ourselves up for failure, but we are denying and dismissing other ways of doing church.

We need a movement of church partnership, and interchurch interaction. White evangelicalism in particular, the tradition I am most familiar with, can get so busy building empires and planting multisite churches that they lose touch with the churches in their own neighborhoods. Christians should attend to Paul's letters in the New Testament, in which he not only wrote to churches across a geographic area but also sent prayers from one church to another. How often do churches, not to mention our pastors, pray for churches in their city and in their nation?

This is especially important when it comes to communication and partnership between churches of different ethnic backgrounds. Across the nation, in pockets of the country, there are signs of what deep church partnership could look like. In my hometown of Buffalo, Protestant churches representing various racial and ethnic groups gather on Good Friday for a citywide service. Tens of thousands of Christians gather to worship under the leadership of diverse worship and teaching and alongside diverse people.

In Richmond, Virginia, there is a consortium of worship musicians who fill in for church worship leaders who cannot make Sunday service. The church will call up the consortium and ask for them to send whoever is available. But here's the thing: the church doesn't know who is coming. A black church might be led in worship that week by an Anglican folk guitar player; a Southern Baptist church might be led by a gospel choir, and through this people truly come to understand what Paul wrote in Galatians: "There is neither Jew nor Gentile, neither slave nor free, nor is there male and female, for you are all one in Christ Jesus."[19]

For those who believe in the Great Commission and heed Jesus' words that we will be known by how we love our fellow believers, the black church should find no better friend than white evangelicalism. What other American community today displays less shame, less reservation, less self-awareness about proclaiming the Christian faith?

Finally, there is a practical reality that should motivate white Christians to address racial inequality in partnership with the black church. Any action in the public square is increasingly ineffective if it comes from only white, conservative evangelical Protestants. There are politicians today, and there will be many more in the future, who do not feel that they *have* to meet with the local evangelical megachurch pastor, but their jobs *depend* on meeting with the influential black pastor in their constituency. White Christians also have much to learn from the experience of the black church, which is familiar with thriving in an antagonistic culture. The pressure of today's societal climate and challenges has the potential to create a new era of church unity.

The gospel, the call of justice, and the demands of our times all call for a concentrated effort at addressing racial injustice and working toward reconciliation. This is a possibility burdened by our history, but enlivened by hope.

Religious Freedom

In recent years, religious freedom has become a controversial topic. Like so many powerful ideas, our politics has reduced it to the subject of fund-raising e-mails and attack ads. As a result, many have tuned out, weary of the culture wars and wary of manipulation. Yet religious freedom is under real pressure, viewed by some as an obstacle to be overcome.

Religious freedom is important because it deals with what is most personal, most unalterable about the human will and conscience. Enshrined in the American constitution's first amendment, the "free exercise" of religion derives from the conviction that gave birth to our nation in the first place: that our rights come from God, not man or his government. The right to believe, worship, and act in light of your faith is one-half of a societal covenant of humility around religion that we make in America. Religious freedom is the government's acknowledgment that its determination of what is right and wrong might be incorrect and therefore should rarely, if ever, intrude upon the individual's right to respond to and follow the commands of his or her religion. Of course, the other side of this covenant is the individual's understanding that even if one is certain in one's religious convictions, one should not seek to have his or her religion favored by government nor to have those of other religions disadvantaged by government due to his or her faith. Together, these ideas provide an elegant framework for interaction between religion and government, believers and their nation.

Today, religious freedom has become a political flash point because it is in tension with government and societal goals around sexuality. How we apply these ideas to the questions of our time will have much to do with the social cohesion of our society in the coming decades. So let me offer a few ideas for consideration as we navigate this difficult terrain:

First, if the free exercise of religion means anything, it is that in all but the most extreme cases, the government should not be in the business of coercing religious institutions to change their beliefs. There is a robust conversation going on in religious communities—Christian, Jewish, and Muslim—on questions of sexual ethics. Religious communities ought to be able to come to determinations about these matters with minimal government pressure or coercion.

Second, to categorically deny federal funding and recognition to any group is to say to them and their fellow citizens that they are not a part of the American family. That they are somehow beneath the nation, unfit to serve their neighbor in partnership with their government. There may be circumstances in which as a nation we might want to send this message, but we should be careful when we do, and keep in mind the social ramifications of doing so.

Finally, religious freedom is important precisely for beliefs that are not popular at the moment. Popular beliefs do not require constitutional protections; they are protected by politics, by the force of popular government. We should have a deep humility when we interfere with religious freedom, precisely because we are injecting the temporal into the eternal. We should remember that religious freedom has allowed for the incubation of the very social progress many of the same people who question religious freedom cherish today. A decade before same-sex marriage was legalized, it was recognized in the American Episcopal Church. When George W. Bush was campaigning for a federal marriage amendment, he did not campaign to revoke the tax status of the Episcopal Church because its views on marriage were "fundamentally un-American." America has benefitted from its commitment to allowing the religious marketplace to operate with minimal interference, and we have come to regret many of the instances where we have turned our backs on it. Religious freedom is a commitment we should continue to uphold.

It was religious freedom that allowed the African Methodist Episcopal Church to form, despite federal laws that treated black people as property, and it was with a restricted conception of religious freedom that North Carolina stopped Quaker communities from emancipating slaves.[20]

For Christians, marriage is primarily a sacred reality, not a legal one. Christian beliefs about marriage cannot be easily separated out from the rest of our faith and lives, nor would we want them to be. The Christian tradition has too much to say to the great confusion and anxiety that permeates our culture on marriage and sexuality.

Now that same-sex marriage is legal, the political debate about it must change because the moral question has changed: to derecognize same-sex marriages would be to break up hundreds of thousands of families by government order. Today, Christians should take up the opportunity granted by our culture's declared affirmation of monogamous, lifelong commitment. Now that everyone can get married, what can we do as a nation to incentivize marriage and help young couples who want to get married but face economic or other hurdles to doing so?[21] We should also revisit the no-fault divorce consensus from the 1980s and have a national conversation about whether that consensus helped or harmed marriage and families.

As we have discussed throughout this book, there is a great incentive in our politics to drive conflict and to make political opponents out to be as extreme as possible. Unless Americans demand from their party's politicians something more than zero-sum politics, that is what we will get on religious freedom issues for the foreseeable future. We need true public servants, statesmen and stateswomen, who recognize that a truly inclusive twenty-first-century America will protect both LGBT rights and religious freedom. At the time of this writing, more than a year after the Supreme Court declared same sex marriage legal, we still do not have federal workplace protections for LGBT Americans. This is not just because of opposition from those who deny that these protections are warranted, but also because of those who will only accept those protections if they do not accommodate religious freedom. We need citizens who see through politicians who claim we can only have one or the other—LGBT rights or religious freedom—and consider not just their own interests but the interests of those they disagree with as well. This will require understanding, imagination, and, yes, hope.

But we ought not reduce questions of religious freedom to conflicts and tensions around issues of sexuality. As previously discussed, the Obama administration rightly and successfully defended the rights of a Muslim retail employee who was fired because her religious attire did not fit her store's dress code and aesthetic. The right of religious communities—Muslim, Christian, Jewish, Buddhist, and others—to have fair access to land and build houses of worship is frequently challenged. Consider also the recent legal issues facing college ministries. On some campuses, Christian student groups have been derecognized because they require the leaders of their organization to be Christian.

When one religious group's freedom is abridged, it affects everyone's religious freedom. Either religious freedom is for all or it is for none. And religious freedom will always be most important to minority religious groups. As with cross-racial solidarity, I believe that Christians should and will consider Muslims, Jewish people, Mormons, and those of other faiths as allies, as people who understand and believe in the importance of a religious conscience, even if their consciences are shaped in different ways. If efforts to advance religious liberty are fought by Christians only, for Christians only, it will be both substantively incoherent and politically ineffective. Christians cannot protest for their religious freedom one day and protest against a mosque opening up down the street the next. Not only does that undermine Christian witness in politics, it undermines religious freedom. Religious freedom is an inclusive principle and therefore must be advanced by an inclusive coalition.

On race, religious freedom, and so many other pressing issues of our day, hope—a hope grounded in the resurrection and the kingdom of God and expressed in our lives through commitment, humility, and the pursuit of justice—is the way forward.

A FINAL WORD TO CHRISTIANS

The days that lie ahead are full of opportunity and potential. God's mercies are new each morning, with each passing day. We will be as we have always been called to be: a witness to His glory and goodness, ambassadors of His love. There truly is no place for fear or anxiety about the future, though we must certainly comfort and encourage one another when the fear and anxiety comes. Rather, we need to act.

In the face of hopelessness, Christians cannot withdraw from their neighbors, under the impression that they are unwanted, and so grant what they think the world wants. We do not love our neighbor for affirmation, but because we have been loved first. Now is not the time to withdraw, but to refine our intentions and pursue public faithfulness that truly *is* good news. Churches should open their doors and seek the answers to the questions their neighbors are asking along with them.

In politics, Christians must think about the institutions we have, the institutions we need, and how to support them. If we want to sustain a culture-conscious political engagement, Christians need to create and support institutions—foundations, advocacy organizations, media projects—that support those who refuse expediency in favor of faithfulness. Politics can be a ministry, and we ought to financially support those in it as we would those serving in other fields.

When I look back at my arrival in Washington, I realize that even if I had the right answers about hope, my heart was confused about what it meant. I thought I knew how God was working, and I was sometimes surprised when things did not go as I had planned. Yet, by His grace I saw Him work in incredible ways during my time with the president. I saw Christians in government and outside of it serve their neighbor with humility, commitment, and faithfulness in pursuit of justice.

And it all pointed to Jesus, in whom hope and history met and gave birth to new history and a new hope. He is the one we can trust. His loving plan will set wrongs to rights. And we have this incredible grace to worship Him with our lives, to join Him in His work, for the good of all of our neighbors of all faiths and backgrounds. We can do all of this with joy, a "pervasive and constant sense of well-being,"[22] whether or not our candidate wins an election, or a policy we disapprove of is enacted. Our goal is not victory, but faithfulness.

This is a time for reclaiming. We must clear out the wreckage from our politics, our relationships, and our hearts. Standing on reclaimed ground, we will look out toward the horizon and see no end to the possibilities.

We can throw off everything that hinders us. We can run the race marked out for us. We can reclaim hope in our time.

ACKNOWLEDGMENTS

This book is the product of much prayer, thought, tears, laughter, reflection, conversation, love, and, yes, hope—all of which are not investments of mine alone, but also family, friends, and colleagues. It is daunting to even think of capturing all the people who provided support, encouragement, and insight to me while writing this book. I can only ask for grace from those I unintentionally leave out.

Melissa, my wife, the vision who captivated me all those years ago, was my essential partner in this book. It was Melissa who provided the confidence to begin this endeavor. It was her wisdom that first sifted the wheat from the chaff, her love that held off overwhelming doubt in the writing process, and her patience that helped her persevere through reading and providing invaluable feedback on draft after draft. The book is dedicated to her and she was at the center of its creation. Our life together is the best of my stories.

ACKNOWLEDGMENTS

To my family, especially my mother, Genevieve; my sister and brother-in-law, Dana and Keith. My in-laws, Jon, Kim, Jon Jr., and Jenna; Angie and Chuck; Jerry and Mary Ann. My cousins Jennifer, Carrie, and Charlie; Larry and Jeanne. My Grandmother and her siblings—Ann, Mariano, and Sara—and their families. And my Papa's siblings—Peter, Angelo, Al, and Nancy—and their families. Thank you for your love, your sacrifices, and your patience with me.

Austin Ricketts served as my invaluable research assistant for this project and the book simply would not have been possible without him. I am grateful for his intellect, pastoral spirit, and enthusiasm. Austin, your insistence that the process of writing this book would be a "journey" and your willingness to travel it with me was a great encouragement.

This book benefitted greatly from several people who provided feedback on drafts of the manuscript and/or proposal, particularly Stephanie Summers, Tyler Wigg-Stevenson, Jonathan Merritt, David Bailey, Patton Dodd, and John Inazu. Your thoughtful engagement with this book strengthened it immeasurably. Just as the book was refined through your influence, I am a better person because of your friendship.

Gabe and Rebekah, your steady friendship has meant the world to me. I am excited for what the future holds for us and this church we love.

Thank you to my church families, including the Chapel at Crosspoint, National Community Church, and Restoration Arlington. Thank you to Jerry Gillis, who first taught me scripture. To Mark Batterson, who baptized me and pastored me through college, the White House, and marriage. And to David Hanke, who we are blessed to have as our pastor today.

ACKNOWLEDGMENTS

So many people encouraged me throughout the writing process and informed the ideas in this book, including Pat MacMillan, Luder Whitlock, Richard Mouw, Joel Hunter, Louie Giglio, Kirsten Powers, Michael Gerson, Pete Wehner, Jason Locy, Russell Moore, Shirley Hoogstra, Shapri LoMaglio, Stanley Carlson-Thies, Galen Carey, Bethany Hoang, Dave and Kate Hodges, Jose and Nikolle Reyes, Jim Daly, Arthur Satterwaite, Art Hooker, Donald Miller, Chris Ferebee, Jason Poling, Jedd Medefind, Bishop Claude Alexander, Francis Davis, and Alan Noble.

Thank you to Tim Keller and N. T. Wright for your time and suggestions at critical moments during the writing process.

It was an honor to serve with so many talented, dedicated colleagues in the Obama Administration and campaigns. I would particularly like to acknowledge those involved with the faith-based initiative and outreach, including Joshua DuBois, Paul Monteiro, Mara Vanderslice Kelly, Ben O'Dell, John Kelly, Alexia Kelley, Max Finberg, Rachel Rose, Ashley Allison, all of the interns who worked with me, and all staff who served in the agency faith-based centers. I would also like to thank Patrick Dillon, Broderick Johnson, Michael Strautmanis, Melody Barnes, Patrick Gaspard, Pete Rouse, Tina Tchen, Carlos Monje, Heather Higginbottom, Cecilia Munoz, Stacy Koo, Scott Buckhout, my Domestic Policy Council colleagues, and so many others I learned from through our work together. Thank you, Mr. President, for the opportunity to serve and for your service to this nation.

Thank you to my agent, David Patterson, who believed in me and this project from the beginning and to the Stuart Krichevsky Agency.

Thank you to my editor, Webster Younce. Webb, you were the only editor I would trust with this book and your incisive judgment and deep intellect were integral to this project. Thank you for your great care with these words that mean so much to me.

A big thank you as well to the entire Thomas Nelson team for investing in this book and making it possible. In particular, thank you to Jeff James, DJ Lipscomb, Tiffany Sawyer, Brigitta Nortker, and Brittany Lassiter for your hard work getting this book to the public.

Chris Roslan, thank you for joining this effort, and for your masterful work conveying to press the message of this book.

Austin Graff and Brannon McAllister, it was an unexpected gift to get to work with you to reach people with this book and I thank you for your partnership.

Papa, who knows where I would be without you. I hope I have made you proud.

Praise God from whom all blessings flow.

ABOUT THE AUTHOR

Michael Wear is the founder of Public Square Strategies LLC, a consulting firm that helps businesses, non-profits, foundations, and Christian organizations at the intersection of faith, politics, and culture. Wear directed faith outreach for President Obama's historic 2012 re-election campaign and was one of the youngest White House staffers in modern American history, leading evangelical outreach and helping manage the White House's engagement on religious and values issues, including adoption and anti-human trafficking efforts. He holds an honorary position at the University of Birmingham's Edward Cadbury Centre for the Public Understanding of Religion and serves on the national board of Bethany Christian Services. He lives with his wife, Melissa, in Washington, DC.

NOTES

PRELUDE

1. "Transcript: Illinois Senate Candidate Barack Obama," *Washington Post*, July 27, 2004, http://www.washingtonpost.com /wp-dyn/articles/A19751–2004Jul27.html.
2. Macon Phillips, "This Is My Hope. This Is My Prayer," The White House blog, February 5, 2009, http://www.whitehouse.gov/blog /2009/02/05/my-hope-my-prayer.

INTRODUCTION

1. Maggie Fox, "Fewer Americans Believe in God—Yet They Still Believe in Afterlife," NBC News, March 21, 2016, http://www .nbcnews.com/health/mental-health/fewer-americans-believe -god-yet-they-still-believe-afterlife-n542966.
2. Chuck Todd, "America: In Search of a Political Reset in 2016," NBC News, November 3, 2015, http://www.nbcnews.com /meet-the-press/america-search-political-reset-2016-n456216.

3. Shanto Iyengar and Sean J. Westwood, "Fear and Loathing across Party Lines: New Evidence on Group Polarization," (research paper, Political Communication Lab of Stanford University), accessed May 22, 2016, https://pcl.stanford.edu/research/2014/iyengar-ajps-group-polarization.pdf.

4. Dictionary.com, s.v. "reclaim," accessed May 20, 2016, www.dictionary.com/browse/reclaim.

CHAPTER 1: FAMILY VALUES

1. George Packer, *The Unwinding: An Inner History of the New America* (New York: Farrar, Straus and Giroux, 2013). It won the National Book Award for Nonfiction.

CHAPTER 2: MEETING BARACK OBAMA

1. David Kinnaman and Gabe Lyons, *unChristian: What a New Generation Really Thinks About Christianity . . . and Why It Matters* (Grand Rapids: Baker Books, 2007).

2. David Campbell, in J. Lui and A. Stern, "American Grace: How Religion Divides and Unites Us," Pew Research Center, accessed July 25, 2016, http://www.pewforum.org/2010/12/16/american-grace-how-religion-divides-and-unites-us/.

3. Jonathan Merritt, "The Religious Right Turns 33: What Have We Learned?" *Atlantic*, June 8, 2012, http://www.theatlantic.com/politics/archive/2012/06/the-religious-right-turns-33-what-have-we-learned/258204/.

4. Tom Skinner, "The U.S. Racial Crisis and World Evangelism," undated speech, Urbana Student Mission Conference, accessed May 22, 2016, 58:11, https://urbana.org/message/us-racial-crisis-and-world-evangelism.

5. Barack Obama, *The Audacity of Hope: Thoughts on Reclaiming*

the American Dream (New York: Crown/Three Rivers Press, 2007), 212.

6. Barack Obama, "Call to Renewal" Keynote Address, Sojourners /Call to Renewal "Building a Covenant for a New America" conference, Washington DC, June 26, 2006, https://sojo.net /articles/transcript-obamas-2006-sojournerscall-renewal -address-faith-and-politics.

7. Obama, *Audacity of Hope*, 203–04.

8. Ibid., 204.

9. Ibid., 205.

10. Ibid.

11. Ibid., 206.

12. Ibid., 208.

13. Ibid., 208.

14. Obama, "Call to Renewal" Keynote Address, Sojourners/Call to Renewal "Building a Covenant for a New America" conference, Washington DC, June 26, 2006, https://sojo.net/articles/transcript -obamas-2006-sojournerscall-renewal-address-faith-and-politics.

15. Ibid.

16. Alexander Mooney, "Evangelist Accuses Obama of 'Distorting' Bible," CNN, June 24, 2008, http://www.cnn.com/2008/POLITICS /06/24/evangelical.vote/.

17. Tim Grieve, "Left Turn at Saddleback Church," *Salon*, December 2, 2006, http://www.salon.com/2006/12/02/obama_155/.

CHAPTER 3: A CAMPAIGN TO BELIEVE IN

1. Eric M. Appleman, "Barack Obama–Organization, Iowa," *Obama for America*, revised January 24, 2009, https://www.gwu.edu /~action/2008/obama/obamaorgia.html.

2. Eric M. Appleman, "Obama for America Iowa Caucus Field

Organization," *Obama for America*, March 5, 2007, https://www
.gwu.edu/~action/2008/obama/obamaiafield.html.

3. David Remnick, *The Bridge: The Life and Rise of Barack Obama* (New York: Alfred A. Knopf, 2010), 175.

4. Ibid., 518–19.

5. Ibid., 521.

6. Barack Obama, "Transcript: Barack Obama's Speech on Race," NPR, March 18, 2008, http://www.npr.org/templates/story/story .php?storyId=88478467.

7. Ibid.

8. David Plouffe, *The Audacity to Win: The Inside Story and Lessons of Barack Obama's Historic Victory* (New York: Viking Adult, 2009), 224.

9. Sarah Posner, "Obama's Somewhat Secret Meeting with Evangelical Pastors," *American Prospect*, June 13, 2008, http:// prospect.org/article/obamas-somewhat-secret-meeting -evangelical-pastors.

10. CNN, "Obama Campaign Rolls out New 'Faith Merchandise'," *Political Ticker* (blog), September 15, 2008, http://politicalticker. blogs.cnn.com/2008/09/15/obama-campaign-rolls-out-new-faith -merchandise/.

11. Jodi Kantor, "The Obamas' Marriage," *New York Times Magazine*, October 26, 2009, from http://www.nytimes.com/2009/11/01 /magazine/01Obama-t.html.

12. Ibid.

13. David Brooks, Jim Lehrer, and Mark Shields, "Shields and Brooks on Changing Political Landscapes in Florida, U.S." PBS News hour, accessed April 19, 2016, http://www.pbs.org/newshour/bb /politics-jan-june10-shieldsbrooks_04-16/.

14. CNN, "CNN Live Event/Special: 'Saddleback Presidential Candidates Forum,' Transcripts, August 16, 2008, http://www .cnn.com/TRANSCRIPTS/0808/16/se.02.html.

15. Ibid.

16. Misleading, but true. There's a family video somewhere of me singing Brian McKnight.

17. Undeniably true. Buffalo is in New York. (This is what politicos call "spin.")

18. Marvin A. McMickle, ed., *The Audacity of Faith: Christian Leaders Reflect on the Election of Barack Obama* (Valley Forge, PA: Judson Press, 2009), xv.

19. A call sheet is a brief memo that provides details and background for a phone call the candidate will make.

20. Barack Obama, "Transcript: 'This Is Your Victory,' Says Obama," speech in Grant Park, Chicago, November 4, 2008, CNN, http:// edition.cnn.com/2008/POLITICS/11/04/obama.transcript/.

21. Ibid.

CHAPTER 4: PRESIDENT OBAMA'S FAITH IN THE WHITE HOUSE (2009–2010)

1. David Samuels, "The Aspiring Novelist Who Became Obama's Foreign-Policy Guru," *New York Times Magazine*, May 5, 2016, http://www.nytimes.com/2016/05/08/magazine/the-aspiring -novelist-who-became-obamas-foreign-policy-guru.html.

2. Pew Research Center, "Media Coverage of the Faith-Based Initiative in the First Six Months of 2001 and 2009," Religion & Public Life, August 12, 2009, http://www.pewforum.org/2009 /08/12/the-starting-line/.

3. Office of Faith-Based and Neighborhood Partnerships, "Policy

Goals—Key Priorities for Faith-based and Neighborhood Partnerships," The White House, accessed July 25, 2016, https://www.whitehouse.gov/administration/eop/ofbnp/policy.

4. David Kuo, *Tempting Faith: An Inside Story of Political Seduction* (New York: Free Press, 2006), 179–80.

5. Pew Research Center, "Religion in Everyday Life," Religion & Public Life, April 12, 2016, http://www.pewforum.org/2016/04/12/religion-in-everyday-life/.

6. Eunice Lim, "White House honors Penn with Interfaith Service Award," *Daily Pennsylvanian*, October 16, 2014, http://www.thedp.com/article/2014/10/penn-honored-as-finalist-in-white-house-interfaith-award.

7. Arne Duncan and Rev. Brenda Girton-Mitchell, "The President's Interfaith and Community Service Campus Challenge Inaugural Report," US Department of Education, September 2013, retrieved June 14, 2016, http://www2.ed.gov/about/inits/list/fbci/campus-challenge-inaugural-years-report.pdf.

8. B. O'Dell, in discussion with author, March 6, 2016.

9. Macon Phillips, "This Is My Hope. This Is My Prayer." The White House blog, February 5, 2009, https://www.whitehouse.gov/blog/2009/02/05/my-hope-my-prayer.

10. Ibid.

11. Barack Obama, "Remarks by the President at the National Prayer Breakfast," The White House, February 4, 2010, https://www.whitehouse.gov/the-press-office/remarks-president-national-prayer-breakfast.

12. Ibid.

13. Ibid.

14. Ibid.

15. Ibid.

16. Ibid.

17. Ibid.

18. Remnick, *The Bridge*, 199–200.

19. Sheryl Gay Stolberg, "To Promote Health Care Plan, Obama Talks about His Own Grandmother," *New York Times*, August 15, 2009, http://www.nytimes.com/2009/08/16/health/policy /16address.html?_r=0.

20. Norm Ornstein, one of the most consistent voices for bipartisanship in Washington, detailed this process brilliantly in the *Atlantic*; see "The Real Story of Obamacare's Birth," July 6, 2015, http://www.theatlantic.com/politics/archive/2015/07/the -real-story-of-obamacares-birth/397742/.

21. "Accomplishments of the Affordable Care Act: A 5th Year Anniversary Report," Domestic Policy Council, Executive Office of the President, March 22, 2015, https://www.whitehouse.gov /sites/default/files/docs/3-22-15_aca_anniversary_report.pdf.

22. HHS Press Office, "20 million people have gained health insurance coverage because of the Affordable Care Act, new estimates show," press release, US Department of Health and Human Services, March 3, 2016, http://www.hhs.gov/about /news/2016/03/03/20-million-people-have-gained-health- insurance-coverage-because-affordable-care-act-new-estimates.

23. Sabrina Tavernise and Robert Gebeloff, "Immigrants, the Poor and Minorities Gain Sharply under Affordable Care Act," *New York Times*, April 17, 2016, http://www.nytimes.com/2016/04/18 /health/immigrants-the-poor-and-minorities-gain-sharply-under -health-act.html.

CHAPTER 5: PRESIDENT OBAMA'S FAITH IN
THE WHITE HOUSE (2011–2012)

1. Pew Research Center, "Growing Number of Americans Say Obama Is a Muslim," Religion & Public Life, August 18, 2010, http://www.pewforum.org/2010/08/18/growing-number-of -americans-say-obama-is-a-muslim/.

2. Or, some would say, "Professor Obama."

3. Mayhill Fowler, "Obama: No Surprise That Hard-Pressed Pennsylvanians Turn Bitter," *Huffington Post*, November 17, 2008, http://www.huffingtonpost.com/mayhill-fowler/obama-no -surprise-that-ha_b_96188.html.

4. David Plouffe, *The Audacity to Win: The Inside Story and Lessons of Barack Obama's Historic Victory* (New York: Viking Adult, 2009), 216. Ibid.

5. Ibid.

6. Ibid.

7. The president loves gospel music and appreciates a church with a good gospel choir. If that choir has a female soloist who can really belt it out, he'll be smiling on his way out of the service and even for the rest of the day.

8. As a matter of press access and government transparency, the president has a selected, rotating group of reporters who follow him to nearly every public event that is held.

9. After a visit to one church, ABC News reported: "Still, not everyone was happy to see all the VIPs. Worshipers were forced to wait in long lines and go through metal detectors, while latecomers were turned away for security reasons. Several were upset about missing holiday services, but preferred not to comment." Yunji Denies and Tom Giusto, "President Obama Attends Easter Service, but Will He Become a Church Regular?"

ABC News, April 4, 2010, http://abcnews.go.com/WN/president -obama-takes-easter-mass-church-regular/story?id=10283263.

10. Joshua DuBois, "Keeping Tabs on Obama's Church Attendance Is No Way to Gauge His Faith," *Daily Beast*, January 5, 2014, http://www.thedailybeast.com/articles/2014/01/05/keeping-tabs-on -obama-s-church-attendance-is-no-way-to-gauge-his-faith.html.

11. Mark Driscoll, on Twitter: "Praying for our president, who today will place his hand on a Bible he does not believe to take an oath to a God he likely does not know," January 21, 2013, https:// twitter.com/pastormark/status/293391878949335043.

12. Barack Obama, "Remarks by the President at National Prayer Breakfast," The White House, February 3, 2011, https://www .whitehouse.gov/the-press-office/2011/02/03/remarks-president -national-prayer-breakfast.

13. Ibid.

14. Ibid.

15. Ibid.

16. For example, see the Catalyst Conference Challenge of 2011, accessed April 21, 2016, http://archive.charitywater.org/catalyst/.

17. "National Prayer Breakfast," February 3, 2011.

18. Ibid.

19. Mollie Hemingway, "Obama's Confession of Faith," *Get Religion*, April 20, 2011, http://www.getreligion.org/getreligion/2011/04 /obamas-confession-of-faith.

20. Barack Obama, "Remarks by the President at Easter Prayer Breakfast," The White House, April 6, 2010, https://www .whitehouse.gov/the-press-office/remarks-president-easter -prayer-breakfast.

21. Barack Obama, "Remarks by the President at the National Prayer Breakfast," The White House, February 2, 2012, https://www

.whitehouse.gov/the-press-office/2012/02/02/remarks-president
-national-prayer-breakfast.

22. Ibid.

23. Ibid.

24. Ibid.

25. Ibid.

26. Ibid.

27. Jonathan Jones, "Pete Souza: Photographing the Real Barack
Obama," *Guardian* (UK), May 29, 2016, http://www.theguardian
.com/artanddesign/2016/may/29/pete-souza-photographing
-the-real-barack-obama.

CHAPTER 6: SEARCHING FOR COMMON GROUND ON ABORTION

1. Kristin Dombek, "'Defenders of the Unborn,' by Daniel K.
Williams," Sunday Book Review, *New York Times*, January 8,
2016, retrieved May 18, 2016, http://www.nytimes.com/2016
/01/10/books/review/defenders-of-the-unborn-by-daniel-k
-williams.html.

2. "The Email Exchange Between a Chicago Doctor and
Then-Senate Candidate Barack Obama," from March 2004,
Washington Post, n.d., accessed April 22, 2016, http://www
.washingtonpost.com/apps/g/page/politics/the-email-exchange
-between-a-chicago-doctor-and-then-senate-candidate-barack
-obama/1918/.

3. Ibid.

4. Ibid.

5. Sarah Pulliam and Ted Olsen, "Q&A: Barack Obama," *Christianity
Today*, January 23, 2008, http://www.christianitytoday.com/ct
/2008/januaryweb-only/104-32.0.html.

6. Terence P. Jeffrey, "Obama Is the Most Pro-Abortion Candidate

Ever," *Human Events*, January 9, 2008, http://humanevents
.com/2008/01/09/obama-is-the-most-proabortion-candidate
-ever/. See also Robert P. George, "Obama's Abortion Extremism,"
Witherspoon Institute Public Discourse, October 14, 2008, http://
www.thepublicdiscourse.com/2008/10/133/.

7. Sara Just, "Obama: Sounding Like Thomas and Scalia?" ABC
News, August 5, 2008, http://blogs.abcnews.com/legalities/2008
/07/obama-sounding.html.

8. Perhaps the most notable example of this was his vote against
the Born-Alive Infant Protection Act. See more: Josh Hicks,
"Did Obama Deny Rights to Infants Who Survive Abortion?"
Washington Post, September 10, 2012, https://www
.washingtonpost.com/blogs/fact-checker/post/did-obama-vote-to
-deny-rights-to-infant-abortion-survivors/2012/09/07/9852895a
-f87d-11e1-8398-0327ab83ab91_blog.html.

9. Barack Obama, "Remarks by the President at Notre Dame
Commencement," The White House, May 17, 2009, https://www
.whitehouse.gov/the-press-office/remarks-president-notre-dame
-commencement.

10. Ibid.

11. Ibid.

12. Yes, we returned to the old language despite the president's Air
Force One decision.

13. WITW staff, "President Obama Cuts Funding for All Abstinence
-Only Sex Education," Women in the World, *New York Times*,
February 18, 2016, http://nytlive.nytimes.com/womenintheworld
/2016/02/18/president-obama-cuts-funding-for-all-abstinence
-only-sex-education/.

14. Christi Parsons and Kathleen Hennessey, "Obama's Search for
'Balance' Defines His Decision-Making," *Los Angeles Times*,

November 2, 2012, http://articles.latimes.com/2012/nov/02
/nation/la-na-obama-decisions-20121102.

15. Office of Management and Budget, "Statement of Administration
Policy: H.R. 36—Pain-Capable Unborn Child Protection Act," The
White House, January 20, 2015, https://www.whitehouse.gov/sites
/default/files/omb/legislative/sap/114/saphr36r_20150120.pdf.

16. LifeSiteNews.com, "Complete Transcript of McCain, Obama
Abortion Debate Remarks," Life Issues Institute, Inc., October 16,
2008, http://www.lifeissues.org/2000/11/debate_transcript/.

17. Rachel K. Jones and Jenna Jerman, "Abortion Incidence and
Service Availability in the United States, 2011," *Perspectives on
Sexual and Reproductive Health* vol. 46, no. 1 (March 2014),
https://www.guttmacher.org/sites/default/files/pdfs/journals
/psrh.46e0414.pdf.

18. Pam Fessler, "Report: Foster Kids Face Tough Times After Age
18," *Morning Edition*, NPR, April 7, 2010, http://www.npr.org
/templates/story/story.php?storyId=125594259.

19. Abby Sewell, "Most L.A. County Youths Held for Prostitution
Come from Foster Care," *Los Angeles Times*, November 27, 2012,
http://articles.latimes.com/2012/nov/27/local/la-me-1128-sex
-trafficking-20121128.

20. Trishula Patel, "At Capitol, a Homecoming for a D.C. Foster Kid,"
Washington Post, August 22, 2013, http://www.washingtonpost
.com/local/20-year-old-intern-from-a-tough-dc-neighborhood
-excels-on-capitol-hill/2013/08/22/17bd1562-0826-11e3-9941
-6711ed662e71_story.html.

21. "The AFCARS Report," US Department of Health and Human
Services Administration for Children and Families, November 2013,
https://www.acf.hhs.gov/sites/default/files/cb/afcarsreport20.pdf.

22. Jennifer Haberkorn and Burgess Everett, "Report: ACA Abortion

Rules Ignored," *Politico*, September 16, 2014, http://www.politico
.com/story/2014/09/gao-report-obamacare-abortion-rules
-ignored-110990.

CHAPTER 7: THE CONTRACEPTION MANDATE

1. Robert Pear, "Officials Consider Requiring Insurers to Offer Free Contraceptives," *New York Times*, February 2, 2011, http://www .nytimes.com/2011/02/03/health/policy/03health.html?_r=0.

2. Ibid.

3. Pam Belluck, "Abortion Qualms on Morning-After Pill May Be Unfounded," *New York Times*, June 5, 2012, http://www.nytimes .com/2012/06/06/health/research/morning-after-pills-dont-block -implantation-science-suggests.html.

4. Robert Pear, "Panel Recommends Coverage for Contraception," *New York Times*, July 19, 2011, http://www.nytimes.com/2011 /07/20/health/policy/20health.html?mtrref=undefined.

5. Christi Parsons and Kathleen Hennessey, "Obama's 'Search for Balance' Defines His Decision-Making," *Los Angeles Times*, November 2, 2012, articles.latimes.com/2012/nov/02/nation /la-na-obama-decisions-20121102.

6. Ibid.

7. Helene Cooper and Laurie Goodstein, "Rule Shift on Birth Control Is Concession to Obama Allies," *New York Times*, February 10, 2012, http://www.nytimes.com/2012/02/11/health /policy/obama-to-offer-accommodation-on-birth-control-rule -officials-say.html?mtrref=undefined.

8. Tim Mak, "Left Blogs Fume over Plan B Decision," *Politico*, December 8, 2011, http://www.politico.com/story/2011/12/left -blogs-fume-over-plan-b-decision-070076.

9. Parsons and Hennessey, "Obama's Search."

10. E. J. Dionne Jr. "Obama's Breach of Faith over Contraceptive Ruling," *Washington Post*, January 29, 2012, https://washingtonpost.com/opinions/obamas-breach-of-faith-over-contraceptive-ruling/2012/01/29/gIQAY7V5aQ_story.html.

11. Parsons and Hennessey, "Obama's Search."

12. Robert Pear, "Obama Reaffirms Insurers Must Cover Contraception," *New York Times*, January 20, 2012, http://www.nytimes.com/2012/01/21/health/policy/administration-rules-insurers-must-cover-contraceptives.html.

13. Ibid.

14. Pear, "Officials Consider."

15. Dionne, "Obama's Breach."

16. Scot McKnight, "Religious Freedom: Under Assault?" *Jesus Creed* (blog), February 29, 2012, http://www.patheos.com/blogs/jesuscreed/2012/02/29/religious-freedom-under-assault/.

17. Monica Schleicher, "Focus' Jim Daly Reserving Final Judgment on Obama Contraception Announcement," press release, Focus on the Family, February 10, 2012, http://www.focusonthefamily.com/about/newsroom/news-releases/20120210-daly-reserving-final-judgment-obama-contraception-announcement.

18. Christi Parsons and Kathleen Hennessey, "Obama Plan Seeks to Defuse Birth Control Debate," *Los Angeles Times*, February 10, 2012, http://articles.latimes.com/2012/feb/10/nation/la-na-contraceptives-fight-20120211.

19. Ibid.

20. Parsons and Hennessey, "Obama's Search."

21. Adam Sorensen, "Conflict over Obama's Contraception Rule Intensifies," *Time*, February 9, 2012, http://swampland.time.com/2012/02/09/conflict-over-obamas-contraception-rule-intensifies/.

22. Barack Obama, "Remarks by the President on Preventive Care," The White House, February 10, 2012, https://www.whitehouse .gov/the-press-office/2012/02/10/remarks-president-preventive -care.

23. Cooper and Goodstein, "Rule Shift."

24. Laurie Goodstein, "Obama Shift on Providing Contraception Splits Critics," *New York Times*, February 14, 2012, http://www .nytimes.com/2012/02/15/us/obama-shift-on-contraception -splits-catholics.html?mtrref=undefined.

25. Laurie Goodstein, "Bishops Reject White House's New Plan on Contraception," *New York Times*, February 11, 2012, http://www .nytimes.com/2012/02/12/us/catholic-bishops-criticize-new -contraception-proposal.html?mtrref=undefined.

26. Alec MacGillis, "On Birth Control, Obama Saved by the Taco Bell?" *New Republic*, February 7, 2012, https://newrepublic.com /article/100577/birth-control-obama-saved-the-taco-bell.

27. Cameron Joseph, "Planned Parenthood Endorses Obama with $1.4 Million Ad Buy," *The Hill*, May 30, 2012, http://thehill.com /video/campaign/229979-planned-parenthood-endorses-obama -launches-14m-ad-buy.

28. Emily Schultheis, "Obama Ad Revives War on Women Theme," *Burns & Haberman Blog*, July 26, 2012, http://www.politico.com /blogs/burns-haberman/2012/07/obama-ad-revives-war-on -women-theme-130207.

29. Parsons and Hennessey, "Obama's Search."

30. Michael Sean Winters, "Sr. Carol Keehan & the HHS Mandate," *National Catholic Reporter*, June 16, 2012, https://www.ncronline .org/blogs/distinctly-catholic/sr-carol-keehan-hhs-mandate.

31. Brian Roewe, "Obama Administration Issues Final Rules on HHS Contraceptive Mandate," *National Catholic Reporter*, June 28,

2013, https://ncronline.org/news/politics/obama-administration
-issues-final-rules-hhs-contraceptive-mandate.

32. Louise Radnofsky, "Obama Administration Offers Contraception
Compromise for Religious Employers," *Wall Street Journal*,
August 22, 2014, http://www.wsj.com/articles/obama
-administration-to-offer-contraception-compromise-for
-religious-employers-1408726941.

33. Sarah Ferris, "Feds Set Final Rules for Birth Control Mandate,"
The Hill, July 10, 2015, http://thehill.com/policy/healthcare
/247507-feds-tweak-obamacare-birth-control-mandate.

34. David Gibson, "Catholic Hospitals and Birth Control: CHA
at Odds with Catholic Bishops on Contraception Mandate,"
Huffington Post, July 10, 2013, http://www.huffingtonpost
.com/2013/07/10/catholic-hospitals-birth-control_n_3568874.html.

35. Eugene Volokh, "More from Michael McConnell on the
Supplementary Briefing in 'Zubik v. Burwell,'" Washington Post,
April 13, 2016, https://www.washingtonpost.com/news
/volokh-conspiracy/wp/2016/04/13/more-from-michael
-mcconnell-on-the-supplementary-briefing-in-zubik-v-burwell
/?postshare=611460581821724.

36. Chris Geidner, "BuzzFeed News Exclusive Interview with
President Obama," BuzzFeed Video, May 16, 2016, https://www
.youtube.com/watch?v=WVqZ269kUr8#t=27m15s.

37. Evan Osnos, "The Biden Agenda," *New Yorker*, July 28, 2014,
http://www.newyorker.com/magazine/2014/07/28/biden-agenda.

38. Greg Jaffe, "The Quiet Impact of Obama's Christian Faith,"
Washington Post, December 22, 2015, http://www.washingtonpost
.com/sf/national/2015/12/22/obama-faith/.

CHAPTER 8: THE PRESIDENT'S "EVOLUTION"

1. Peter Hamby, "Obama's Gospel Concerts Raise Hornet's Nest of a Dilemma," CNN, October 27, 2007, http://www.cnn.com/2007 /POLITICS/10/27/obama.gospel/.

2. Joel C. Hunter, Bob Roberts Jr., and Gabriel Salguero, "Come Let Us Reason Together," undated pamphlet, Third Way, accessed April 22, 2016, http://content.thirdway.org/publications/233 /pastor_guide_electronic_final.pdf.

3. "Saddleback Presidential Candidates Forum," transcript, CNN Live Event/Special, August 16, 2008, http://www.cnn.com /TRANSCRIPTS/0808/16/se.02.html.

4. "Obama: 'Marriage Is Not a Civil Right,'" YouTube video, 1:20, 2004 Illinois Senate debate moderated by Alan Keyes, posted by Hunter Stuart, May 16, 2012, https://www.youtube.com/watch?v =c47JlBJDBVo.

5. Barack Obama, *The Audacity of Hope: Thoughts on Reclaiming the American Dream* (New York: Crown/Three Rivers Press, 2007), 222.

6. Chris Harris, "Barack Obama Answers Your Questions About Gay Marriage, Paying For College, More," MTV News, November 1, 2008, http://www.mtv.com/news/1598407/barack-obama -answers-your-questions-about-gay-marriage-paying-for-college -more/.

7. Sam Stein and Amanda Terkel, "16 Times the Obama Administration Lied About the President's Position on Same-Sex Marriage," *Huffington Post*, February 10, 2015, http://www .huffingtonpost.com/2015/02/10/obama-same-sex-marriage _n_6652892.html.

8. Andrew Sullivan, "David Plouffe on Becker's Book: 'Decidedly Inaccurate,'" *The Dish* (blog, now inactive), April 22, 2014, http://dish.andrewsullivan.com/2014/04/22/david-plouffe-on-beckers-book-decidedy-inaccurate/.

9. ABC News, "Transcript: Robin Roberts ABC News Interview with President Obama," ABC News, May 9, 2012, http://abcnews.go.com/Politics/transcript-robin-roberts-abc-news-interview-president-obama/story?id=16316043.

10. What "neighbors" did he speak to over the past several years while living at the White House?

11. ABC News, "Transcript: Robin Roberts . . . President Obama."

12. Ibid.

13. Ibid.

14. "Winning at the Ballot" (strategy statement, undated), Freedom to Marry (political action campaign, now defunct), accessed April 22, 2016, http:// www.freedomtomarry.org/pages/Winning-at-the-Ballot.

15. ABC News, "Transcript: Robin Roberts . . . President Obama."

16. Brian Montopoli, "Gay Rights in Spotlight at Democratic Convention," CBS News, September 5, 2012, http://www.cbsnews.com/news/gay-rights-in-spotlight-at-democratic-convention/.

17. David Axelrod, *Believer: My Forty Years in Politics* (New York: Penguin Press, 2015), 447.

18. Stein and Terkel, "16 Times."

19. President Obama would host a screening of Steven Spielberg's movie "Lincoln" at the White House in November 2012. (http://www.cbsnews.com/news/president-obama-to-host-white-house-screening-of-lincoln/) And, oddly enough, Hillary Clinton would point to the same film when asked in the second presidential debate in 2016 about leaked transcripts where she spoke about

the need to sometimes have a different position in public than in private. (http://www.nytimes.com/2016/10/10/us/politics /transcript-second-debate.html?_r=0)

20. Buzzfeed Staff, "Full Transcript of Buzzfeed News' Interview with President Barack Obama," Buzzfeed News, February 10, 2015, https://www.buzzfeed.com/buzzfeednews/full-transcript-of -buzzfeed-news-interview-with-president?utm_term= .uoRQBNkzQ#.ydyA5zjmA.

21. Alexandra Jaffe, "Axelrod Explains Obama on Gay Marriage: 'Leaders Work This Way,'" CNN, February 12, 2015, http://www .cnn.com/2015/02/11/obama-david-axelrod-interview/.

22. Sullivan, "David Plouffe on Becker's Book."

23. Juliet Eilperin and Greg Jaffe, "From Obama, a More Confident Tone," *Washington Post*, June 27, 2015, https://www.washingtonpost .com/politics/from-obama-a-more-confident-tone-emerges/2015/06 /27/fa66cf0e-1ce0-11e5-ab92-c75ae6ab94b5_story.html.

24. Chris Hayes, "Axelrod: Obama Misled Public on Gay Marriage," All In with Chris Hayes, MSNBC, February 10, 2015, http://www .msnbc.com/all-in/watch/axelrod--obama-misled-public-on-gay -marriage-397083715521.

25. Ibid.

26. Ibid.

27. Hayes, "Axelrod: Obama Misled Public."

28. "Analysis of National Post-Election Survey and State Exit Surveys on Marriage Equality," Greenberg Quinlan Rosner Research, December 3, 2012, http://www.gqrr.com/articles/2012/12/04 /analysis-of-national-post-election-survey-and-state-exit-surveys -on-marriage-equality.

29. Ben Smith, "Obama Backed Same-Sex Marriage in 1996," *Ben Smith Blog*, January 13, 2009, http://www.politico.com/blogs

/ben-smith/2009/01/obama-backed-same-sex-marriage-in-1996
-015306.

CHAPTER 9: A DIFFERENT KIND OF CAMPAIGN

1. Nick Donnelly, "Obama Hires Apostate Catholic to Counter Catholic Bishops Campaign," *Protect the Pope* (blog), May 15, 2012, http://protectthepope.com/?p=5196.

2. Napp Nazworth, "Obama Praises Bush as 'Man of Faith,'" CP Politics, *Christian Post*, August 21, 2012, http://www .christianpost.com/news/obama-praises-bush-as-man-of-faith -80354/.

3. Eleanor Clift, "Democrats Push Envelope on Abortion, Drop Insistence That It Be Rare," *Daily Beast*, September 15, 2012, http://www.thedailybeast.com/articles/2012/09/15/democrats -push-envelope-on-abortion-drop-insistence-that-it-be-rare.html.

4. Emily Friedman, "Mitt Romney Vows God Will Stay in GOP Platform," ABC News, September 8, 2012, http://abcnews.go.com /blogs/politics/2012/09/mitt-romney-vows-god-will-stay-in-gop -platform.

5. Mojo news team, "Full Transcript of the Mitt Romney Secret Video," *Mother Jones*, September 19, 2012, http://www .motherjones.com/politics/2012/09/full-transcript-mitt-romney -secret-video.

6. Charlie Spiering, "Obama Campaign: Profanity a Hit in Fundraising Emails," *Washington Examiner*, November 29, 2012, http://www.washingtonexaminer.com/obama-campaign -profanity-a-hit-in-fundraising-emails/article/2514675.

7. Jennifer Steinhauer, "Democrats Hand Victory to Obama on Iran Nuclear Deal," *New York Times*, September 10, 2015, http://www

.nytimes.com/2015/09/11/us/politics/iran-nuclear-deal-senate.
html?_r=0.

8. Noam Scheiber, "The Obama Whisperer," *New Republic*,
November 9, 2014, https://newrepublic.com/article/120170
/valerie-jarrett-obama-whisperer.

9. Hunter Schwarz, "Did You Hear the One about the Muslim,
Socialist, Kenyan President? The Joke Obama Can't Stop Telling,"
Washington Post, April 26, 2015, https://www.washingtonpost
.com/news/the-fix/wp/2015/04/26/obama-jokes-about-being-a
-socialist-kenya-born-muslim-at-every-whcd/.

10. Maggie Haberman, "Seeing Likely Nominee, Hillary Clinton Hits
Jeb Bush Hard," *New York Times*, August 5, 2015, http://www
.nytimes.com/2015/08/06/us/politics/seeing-likely-nominee
-hillary-clinton-hits-jeb-bush-hard.html?nytmobile=0.

11. Reid Cherlin, "The Presidency and the Press," *Rolling Stone*,
August 4, 2014, http://www.rollingstone.com/politics/news
/the-presidency-and-the-press-20140804.

12. Barack Obama, "Remarks of President Barack Obama—State of
the Union Address as Delivered," The White House, January 13,
2016, https://www.whitehouse.gov/the-press-office/2016/01/12
/remarks-president--%E2%80%93-prepared-delivery-state-union
-address.

13. Clifton B. Parker, "Political Animosity Exceeds Racial Hostility,
New Stanford Research Shows," Stanford News, Stanford
University, October 8, 2014, http://news.stanford.edu/news/2014
/october/dems-gop-polarized-10–08–14.html.

14. Ray LaHood and Frank H. Mackaman, *Seeking Bipartisanship:
My Life in Politics* (Amherst, NY: Cambria Press, 2015), 286.

15. Ibid., 287.

CHAPTER 10: THE TALE OF TWO INAUGURALS

1. "Rick Warren to Give Invocation at Obama's Inauguration; Update: Gay Groups Go Ballistic," *Hot Air*, December 17, 2008, http://hotair.com/archives/2008/12/17/rick-warren-to-give-invocation-at-obamas-inauguration.

2. Nia-Malika Henderson and Ben Smith, "Gay Leaders Furious with Obama," *Politico*, December 17, 2008, http://www.politico.com/story/2008/12/gay-leaders-furious-with-obama-016693?o=1.

3. Ibid., http://www.politico.com/story/2008/12/gay-leaders-furious-with-obama-016693?o=0.

4. Alexander Mooney, Rebecca Sinderbrand, and John Helton, "Obama: Choice of Warren Reflects Diversity of Ideas," CNN, December 18, 2008, http://www.cnn.com/2008/POLITICS/12/18/obama.warren/.

5. Susan Donaldson James, "Pastor Warren Sets Inclusive Tone at Inaugural," ABC News, January 20, 2009, http://abcnews.go.com/Politics/Inauguration/rick-warren-invocation-president-obama-inauguration/story?id=6687731.

6. Tobin Harshaw, "Invoking Rick Warren," op-ed, *New York Times*, January 20, 2009, http://opinionator.blogs.nytimes.com/2009/01/20/invoking-rick-warren/?_r=0.

7. "Inaugural Benediction to be Delivered By Pastor Who Gave Vehemently Anti-Gay Sermon," *ThinkProgress* (blog), January 9, 2013, retrieved July 25, 2016, https://thinkprogress.org/lgbt/2013/01/09/1422021/inaugural-benediction-to-be-delivered-by-anti-gay-pastor/inaugural-benediction-to-be-delivered-by-pastor-who-gave-vehemently-anti-gay-sermon-e58c9362c949#.qrdxx6wo6.

8. It is worth noting that he delivered this sermon at about the same time Democrats were voting for "don't ask, don't tell" and the Defense of Marriage Act.

9. Lyons and Keller's participation in the meeting was discussed in Lyons and David Kinnaman's book, *Good Faith: Being a Christian When Society Thinks You're Irrelevant and Extreme* (Grand Rapids: Baker Books, 2016).

10. Jeff Zeleny and David D. Kirkpatrick, "Obama's Choice of Pastor Creates Furor," *New York Times*, December 19, 2008, http://www .nytimes.com/2008/12/20/us/politics/20warren.html?_r=0.

11. Neela Banerjee, "Pastor Pulls out of Obama Inauguration Benediction," *Los Angeles Times*, January 10, 2013, http://articles .latimes.com/2013/jan/10/nation/la-na-inaugural-pastor-20130111.

CHAPTER 11: REAL HOPE

1. Josef Pieper, *Hope and History: Five Salzburg Lectures* (San Francisco, CA: Ignatius Press, 1994), 28.

2. Ta-Nehisi Coates, *Between the World and Me* (New York: Spiegel & Grau, 2015), pp. 70–71.

3. Conservative Andre Archie wrote that Coates "attempts to speak truth to power but instead speaks defeatism and a warped view of America to a son" in "The Hopeless Politics of Ta-Nehisi Coates," *American Conservative*, retrieved May 22, 2016, http://www .theamericanconservative.com/articles/the-hopeless-politics-of-ta -nehisi-coates/.

4. *New York Times* op-ed columnist David Brooks argued that the American dream, which Coates rejects, "is a secular faith that has unified people across every known divide. It has unleashed ennobling energies and mobilized heroic social reform movements. By dissolving the dream under the acid of an excessive realism, you trap generations in the past and destroy the guiding star that points to a better future." Read more in "Listening to Ta-Nehisi Coates While White," *New York Times*,

July 17, 2015, http://www.nytimes.com/2015/07/17/opinion /listening-to-ta-nehisi-coates-while-white.html.

5. Michelle Alexander, "Ta-Nehisi Coates's 'Between the World and Me,'" Sunday Book Review, *New York Times*, August 17, 2015, http://www.nytimes.com/2015/08/17/books/review/ta-nehisi -coates-between-the-world-and-me.html.

6. Ta-Nehisi Coates, "Hope and the Historian," *Atlantic*, December 10, 2015, http://www.theatlantic.com/politics/archive/2015/12 /hope-and-the-historian/419961/.

7. Theodore Parker, *Ten Sermons of Religion* (Boston: Crosby, Nichols, 1853), on Google Books, retrieved July 11, 2016, https:// books.google.com/books?id=sUUQAAAAYAAJ&.

8. Martin Luther King Jr., "The Christian Way of Life in Human Relations" (address delivered at the General Assembly of the National Council of Churches, December 4, 1957, St. Louis, MO), King Encyclopedia, Stanford University, accessed July 11, 2016, http://kingencyclopedia.stanford.edu/encyclopedia/documentsentry /the_christian_way_of_life_in_human_relations.1.html.

9. Anthony A. Hoekema, *The Bible and the Future* (Grand Rapids: Eerdmans, 1979), 45.

10. Thabiti Anyabwile, "A Call for Hope in the Age of Mass Incarceration," *Atlantic*, September 15, 2015, http://www. theatlantic.com/politics/archive/2015/09/why-there-needs-to -be-more-hope/404977/.

11. Ibid.

12. Nicola A. Menzie, "Pastor Thabiti Anyabwile Makes the Case for Hope at 'Race and Justice in America' *Atlantic* Summit," Nicola A. Menzie Online, November 12, 2015, http://www .nicolamenzieonline.com/pastor-thabiti-anyabwile-makes-the

-case-for-hope-at-race-and-justice-in-america-atlantic-summit,
page no longer accessible.

13. Ibid.

14. Ibid.

15. Ibid.

16. Ibid.

17. Ibid.

18. Jürgen Moltmann, *Theology of Hope*, 1st Fortress Press ed.
(Minneapolis: Fortress, 1993), 32.

19. Raphael Warnock, "Dreams from Our Fathers," in *The Audacity
of Faith: Christian Leaders Reflect on the Election of Barack
Obama*, ed. M. A. McMickle (Valley Forge, PA: Judson Press,
2009), 65.

CHAPTER 12: RECLAIMING HOPE

1. Ray LaHood and Frank H. Mackaman, *Seeking Bipartisanship:
My Life in Politics* (Amherst, NY: Cambria Press, 2015), 207.

2. Evan Osnos, "In the Land of the Possible," *New Yorker*, December
22, 29, 2014, http://www.newyorker.com/magazine/2014/12/22
/land-possible.

3. Ibid.

4. Jeremiah 29:7 NIV.

5. Luke 4:18–19 NIV.

6. Matthew 5:13–16 NIV.

7. Jeffrey M. Jones, "In U.S., New Record 43% Are Political
Independents," Gallup Poll Social Series, January 7, 2015, http://
www.gallup.com/poll/180440/new-record-political-independents
.aspx.

8. "Millennials in Adulthood," Pew Research Center, March 7, 2014,

http://www.pewsocialtrends.org/2014/03/07/millennials-in
-adulthood/.

9. John R. W. Stott, *The Message of the Sermon on the Mount:
Christian Counter-Culture* (Downers Grove, IL: InterVarsity
Press, 1992), 65.

10. "Poverty: Overview," Topics, *World Bank*, last updated April 13,
2016, http://www.worldbank.org/en/topic/poverty/overview.

11. "World Bank Forecasts Global Poverty to Fall Below 10% for First
Time; Major Hurdles Remain in Goal to End Poverty by 2030,"
press release, *World Bank*, October 4, 2015, retrieved March 21,
2016, www.worldbank.org/en/news/press-release/2015/10/04
/world-bank-forecasts-global-poverty-to-fall-below-10-for-first
-time-major-hurdles-remain-in-goal-to-end-poverty-by-2030.

12. C. S. Lewis, "Meditation on the Third Commandment,"
Guardian (UK), January 10, 1941, 18.

13. Jeff Guo, "America Has Locked Up So Many Black People It Has
Warped Our Sense of Reality," *Washington Post*, February 26,
2016, https://www.washingtonpost.com/news/wonk/wp/2016
/02/26/america-has-locked-up-so-many-black-people-it-has
-warped-our-sense-of-reality/.

14. Bryan Stevenson, "We Need to Talk about an Injustice,"
transcript, TED talk, March 2012, https://www.ted.com/talks
/bryan_stevenson_we_need_to_talk_about_an_injustice
/transcript?language=en.

15. Lindsey Cook, "US Education: Still Separate and Unequal," *US
News & World Report*, January 28, 2015, http://www.usnews.com
/news/blogs/data-mine/2015/01/28/us-education-still-separate
-and-unequal.

16. "African Americans," The State of Working America, 12th Edition, Economic Policy Institute, 2012, accessed May 3, 2016, http://stateofworkingamerica.org/fact-sheets/african-americans/.

17. Emery P. Dalesio and Jonathan Drew, "Appeals Court: North Carolina Voter ID Law Unconstitutional," *Washington Post*, July 30, 2016, https://www.washingtonpost.com/national/appeals -court-north-carolina-voter-id-law-unconstitutional/2016 /07/30/9b5f7296-5627-11e6-b652-315ae5d4d4dd_story.html.

18. Ta-Nehisi Coates, "The Case for Reparations," *Atlantic*, June 2014, https://www.theatlantic.com/magazine/archive/2014/06 /the-case-for-reparations/361631/.

19. Galatians 3:28 NIV.

20. Erasmus, "Church, State, and Early America: Breaches in the Wall of Separation," *The Economist*, August 2015, http://www .economist.com/blogs/erasmus/2015/08/church-state-and-early -america.

21. I discussed this question in more detail in "The American Family Is Making a Comeback," *Atlantic*, October 1, 2014, https://www .theatlantic.com/politics/archive/2014/10/the-family-is-making -a-comeback/380956/.

22. Dallas Willard, *The Great Omission: Reclaiming Jesus's Essential Teachings on Discipleship* (New York: HarperCollins, 2014), 128.

INDEX

INDEX